BRUTALLY HONEST:
MEMOIRS OF A SUICIDER

KEVIN A.J HANNA

Further, Kevin A.J Hanna is not a licensed health professional and offers EFT Tapping as a Personal Performance Coach. This book is intended for information purposes only and is not intended to substitute medical advice. The author does not dispense medical advice or prescribe the use of any technique as a form of treatment for physical or medical problems, without the advice of a physician, either directly or indirectly. The author's intent is only to offer information of a general nature to help you in your quest for spiritual and emotional wellbeing. In the event that you use any of the information in this book for yourself, which is your constitutional right, the author assumes no responsibility for your actions.

CAUTIONARY NOTICE AND DISCLAIMER

Please be advised that the following pages contain sensitive matter related to but not limited to self-harm, sexual abuse, violence, religion and suicidal tendencies. The language and jargon used are that of the author and contains explicit and "foul language".

Those who may be hyper-sensitive to any of the above are advised to proceed with caution.

ACKNOWLEDGEMENT AND DEDICATION

Now completing these memoires and sharing them with the world many years after the fact, there is a veritable plethora of individuals, acquaintances, bullies, lost loves and teachers I could easily acknowledge for their roles in my life and will in the future release.

However, I am dedicating these memoires to every person that has, does or will struggle with suicidal tendencies, extreme guilt and crippling shame. Regardless of how you have come across these words, please know that you are not alone, have never been alone, nor ever will be alone.

None of what you may be experiencing is your fault.

I am only a whisper and a breath away.

Kevin

FORWARD

This book has been many years in the making, as it took an entire lifetime to come to grips with the events that happened in my life. The life within these pages was not rehearsed or fabricated but my reality.

During my life, I have accumulated so much baggage and stress that the burden of the weight was too strenuous. I have known or had 'messages' for over the last two decades that putting my life on paper would be something I could not avoid, and it has been that long that I have procrastinated this healing process.

As I begin to take you on this journey, this personal healing journey, know that I expect nothing in return from you, the reader. At times, you may think I am twisted or psychotic. You may experience feelings of anger or resentment towards me, or you may sympathize with me. However, you react, understand that this is part of my healing journey.

There will be times during the course of this journey that my own personal traumas will resurface, taking me back to times of devastating grief, sorrow and loss, possibly even retraumatization. Emotions of anger, resentment and hostility will also show their ugly heads. I am prepared, however, to let it all out because I know within my heart that this is what I am being inspired to do.

Maybe this journey of atonement will allow you to acknowledge, accept, forgive, and release past personal traumas as well.

INTRODUCTION

For generations, Victorian lineage families, dating back as far as the early 1800s, raised children to be quiet and "well-behaved" according to traditional Victorian standards. This sentiment was widespread during the Victorian era (1837 to 1901) when typical families had about a dozen children. According to the University of Liverpool, the idea that children had no voice persisted well into the 20th century. This was certainly the case with my upbringing and my entire paternal lineage.

With the help of a dear cousin, we have traced my grandmother's lineage back over two centuries, uncovering several high-ranking Masons, among other things, and are still tracing my grandfather's lineage. A significant influence on my father's upbringing—and his father's was a strong British military background that extended over several generations. This form of indoctrination was inevitable for me and my siblings, and its repercussions proved quite destructive over time.

Victorian-era rules and values dictated that every aspect of a child's life should be controlled by their parents or guardians. During this period, little distinction was made between children and property, meaning children were expected to be silent and obedient, following orders without question.

However, the belief that children's words, thoughts, or opinions were unimportant predates the Victorian era. John Locke, in his 1690 work "An Essay Concerning Human Understanding," introduced the idea of "Tabula Rasa" (Latin for "Blank Slate"), suggesting that a child's mind was a blank slate devoid of reason, knowledge, and experience. Children were therefore not considered capable of having valid opinions or original thoughts and were discouraged from speaking openly in the presence of adults.

Above all, children were judged on perfect manners and behavior. A Victorian tale titled "Table Rules for Little Folks" instructs children to "sit still, be patient, not speak a useless word, be polite and clean, and leave quietly when meals are over." These were certainly the rules in my upbringing during the 60s in Eastern Ontario.

One absolute truth I've learned the hard way is that you can have your own opinions but not your own facts. This is undeniable regardless of upbringing, heritage, nationality, or other factors in life. Here are some facts that may sound simple but are often overlooked:

The human mind is an "empty slate" at birth and is influenced without question or restriction until the age of 5-7.

The human mind consists of two key components: the Conscious Mind and the Subconscious Mind.

The Subconscious Mind accepts all information delivered to it repeatedly without hindrance.

A child's basic instincts calls for food, protection, and guidance from parents or guardians.

From birth until early childhood, we have no control over what we are 'fed' into our developing minds. We absorb rules and beliefs without questioning them, as doing so would result in disciplinary actions. Although the intentions of our elders may be innocent, the limitations they impose can stifle proper development, understanding, and self-love, potentially leading to significant personal issues.

I'm not claiming to have had a bad or corrupted childhood; on the contrary. As a young family in 'small-ville' Whitby, Ontario, we never lacked food, shelter, or clean water, and I don't remember being in any real danger. My parents were neither alcoholics, drug addicts, criminals, nor unemployed. We lived such a sheltered life that I didn't even know what a hippie was until the 70s.

I remember my mother working multiple jobs until my younger sister Alison was born, after which she stayed home to raise us. My father worked at a local funeral home for several years before moving into a sales position in Toronto. At a young and impressionable age, I didn't understand what a funeral home was or what my father did there. I do remember the 60's ambulance and hearse often parked in our driveway, the same type used in "Ghostbusters" and "The Addams Family." Perhaps this is why few neighborhood children visited me—they were too creeped out.

Life was simple in our sheltered world, or perhaps I was simply sheltered from the broader world. Every Sunday, we attended the local United Church, where my siblings and I went to Sunday School while our parents remained upstairs. Each week started and ended the same: with the "Lord's Prayer" in the morning and "Now I Lay Me Down to Sleep" at bedtime. Though I was too young to understand it fully, I knew that being "a good boy" was essential to avoid Divine punishment.

Growing up as a Canadian in the 60s, with our black-and-white TV, I recall milestones like the debut of "The Flintstones," "I Love Lucy," "The Dick Van Dyke Show," and "Sesame Street." On the music scene, The Beatles were a screaming success and The Beach Boys were making waves in the U.S. Two significant events I remember, though they didn't fully impact me until later, were the assassination of John F. Kennedy and Martin Luther King's "I Have A Dream" speech. Even as a child, I understood that killing someone because they were different was wrong.

Politically, Canada's landscape was shifting. The British Loyalists, or Tories, who had dominated Parliament, were eventually overtaken by a rising opposition. Meanwhile, in the US, events like the Vietnam War, Civil Rights Protests, the Cuban Missile Crisis, Richard Nixon and Watergate, and the death of Marilyn Monroe shaped the world. The 60s also saw cultural milestones like Woodstock, Bob Dylan, John Lennon, Yoko Ono, and Twiggy's iconic miniskirt. However, these events were censored from our family life, and I think that was justified.

I cannot imagine growing up amid fears of racial persecution or violence. The injustices faced by Aboriginal Peoples in Canada under the Indian Act of 1876 are beyond my comprehension and these injustices still occur in present day times. In my sheltered world, there were only two-family vows: "Be seen and not heard, don't speak unless spoken to," and "Be a good boy, or God will smite you down and send you to Hell." By the age of eleven, I felt destined to burn for an eternity in Hell.

CONTENTS

Acknowledgement and Dedication iii

Forward iv

Introduction v

Chapter 1 1

Chapter 2 7

Chapter 3 12

Chapter 4 20

Chapter 5 32

Chapter 6 42

Chapter 7 64

Chapter 8 75

Chapter 9 85

Chapter 10 91

Chapter 11 96

Chapter 12 105

Chapter 13 125

Chapter 14 134

Chapter 15 140

Summary 147

Closing 157

CHAPTER 1

On September 27th, 1963, Lloyd and Beth Hanna announced to the world the birth of their second son, Kevin Arthur James. I was born in the Oshawa General Hospital and we were currently living in a neighboring town called Whitby. Looking back today, Whitby appears to have changed from a picturesque town to a suburb of Toronto.

Life was pretty simple then; Mom and Dad both worked various jobs, and we moved homes four times within the first several years of my life. Each move seemed to be a step up. By this time, Dad had secured a position with a local Funeral Home, which included driving an ambulance. I was never really sure what he did as work, but I knew it had to do with people who were either sick or dead. The thought of this used to give me the creeps!

During those first few years, several things stuck out very clearly in my mind to this day. One, I can remember riding on the back of my father's motorcycle on a beautiful sunny day. Now understand, I have never seen any pictures whatsoever of my father with a motorcycle. When I posed the question about the motorcycle to my father, he simply laughed and went on to state that "yes," he did own a motorcycle, but it was before I was born. Is that freaky or what?

The next thing I remember was riding my tricycle on the sidewalk outside our home when a storm came up. I don't know if my folks will vouch for this or not, but I distinctly remember that tricycle being hit by some kind of electrical shock with me on it! Why was I not seriously injured? Why don't my parents remember this? Was I dreaming it happened or did I see it happen but to someone else?

The most vivid of all memories deals with experiencing my sexuality as a young boy. I was no more than five years old when I experienced a change in my teeny tiny penis from soft to hard without any control. I soon found out that I was never to talk about it, touch it, or show it – period. Now, I don't care who you are or where you come from; all boys go through this discovery. Touching, feeling, and wondering why it does what it does is normal exploration. My father, on the other hand, apparently didn't believe this was normal and natural because he continuously told me it was a sin of the flesh, unholy, and that if I did not stop touching my penis, he would take the butcher knife and cut it off! Ouch!! Needless to say, I was now terrified to experience my physical body and was branded with someone else's belief that touching my penis was unnatural and unholy. This did not stop me, however, as I just stayed clear of my father.

"Unholy"—what a powerful word that has the ability to induce mental trauma lasting a lifetime. Mom and Dad have always been religious, and they have always worked to instill strong morals and values in us kids. I have no qualms about this, but this Christian upbringing eventually led me to believe that if I was not perfect like

Jesus, God would send me to Hell. This belief was instilled through the church system. It's no wonder that I always felt uncomfortable going to church, as the bar of perfection seemed unattainable.

Now that I was experiencing "me" and how God made me, the next question was how girls were made. This was a simple question to answer because my best friend, who lived just around the corner, was a girl, and surprisingly enough, she was just as curious as I was. This was obviously innocent adolescence, but not according to our parents.

She and I would go skinny dipping for turtles and tadpoles at the local pond and had tons of fun doing it. There was no sexual contact of any kind between us, but I remember feeling the wrath of our parents for playing naked with another child, and this was during the late '60s! Think about this for a minute: we're talking about an era of peace and love, Woodstock and protests, and here I am being punished for being a normal child, and if I did not stop, God would send me straight to Hell!

My guess is that my parents were brought up in a very similar nature with very similar beliefs by their parents. This doesn't make things wrong; it simply means that beliefs that were developed generations ago were never altered or changed but continued to be passed down through the genealogy of the Hanna/Dean family trees. Who knows, maybe hundreds of years ago, they cut off penises or cast children out as witches for exhibiting "Unholy Sexual Behavior."

My early childhood was not Hell on Earth, and I hope I haven't made that impression. We always had food and shelter and weren't sexually or physically abused. Every year, we had family vacations and outings and did many things as a family. I played soccer, then later hockey and baseball. Both myself and older brother Stephen, plus soon to come younger brother Philip, were involved in Boy Scouts. Adolescent life in our family was normal at that time.

In primary school, I proved to be academically inclined, which I probably got from my father. To me, Dad was the smartest and most honest man on the planet. I idolized my father because he had what I wanted – brains, integrity, loyalty, and, very soon, tremendous career success. As a result of seeing this growth in my father, I soon discovered money and made the conscious decision that someday I would be very wealthy. By the age of 7, we had a nice home and a big houseboat. We were successful in my eyes! Dad smoked a pipe as successful men do, and life was grand. I started to look at ways that I could make money and be successful, like my Dad. It wasn't long before I had a paper route of 200 customers and was doing odd jobs for the neighbors as well as around the house. The paper route paid $2 per week, along with an additional $0.10 here and $ 0.75 there from odd jobs. I had become a 7-year-old businessman and was well on my way to becoming wealthy! The accumulation of money was now my main objective, just like it was for my father.

The lesson I did not learn at that age, however, is what money really is and that to be wealthy, you had to save and invest your money. On the other hand, I was more interested in candies and junk because I knew that if I could make money that easily, then all I had to do was keep working, and the money would never stop coming in. The concept of interest and residual income wasn't even a subject open to discussion because it wasn't polite to talk about money or to talk about "adult subjects" of any nature. As a child, I was to "Be seen and not heard, Kevin, don't speak unless you are spoken to, and we do not speak openly about money with children."

My father had changed his position from dead or injured people to a salesman for a leading safety company. This meant more income at the price of extended travel. Since I was to be just like dear old Dad, I accompanied him on some of his business trips. This was very exciting because I got to see my father in action. The better Dad became, the higher up the ladder he climbed. This also meant a lot more travel away from home. Sure, we started to have all the amenities, but where was Dad? Since taking that position until the day I moved out, I cannot honestly remember spending my birthday at home with my father. Dad would call from wherever he was and wish me all the best, but somehow, I was beginning to feel abandoned, as though work was more important than me.

Come late Spring that year, we became a family of five as Mom gave birth to another little boy whom they named Philip. I was 5 when Philip was born, so this made me the middle child, which meant much of the 'allowable affection' shifted to either Stephen as the oldest or Philip as the youngest. Dad had Stephen, and Mom had Philip. I remember Stephen and Dad purchasing a small sailboat and spending weekends floating in the Whitby harbor. As for Mom, well, Philip, being the youngest, required her undivided attention. Love and attention seemed to be fading from my direction. It was attention and pride that drove me to work for money, which made me believe that if I excelled, then love would again come my way. I did everything possible to be the best I could in school while doing as much as possible around the house, thinking that this would 'buy' me the love and attention I was craving. This belief carried on for several more years, then a little sister was brought home on May 10th, 1972. Alison was the newest and last addition to our family.

Alison was more than special to me. She posed no threat to me when it came to missing out on the physical affection of my parents. Sure, Alison was the baby of the family and was adorned by my parents, but by now, I felt as though things would never change and I would never receive the physical love I was so desperately crying out for. Stephen was a constant threat to me as his favorite pastime was pestering me, and Philip became just another member of the family. As I think about it now, the physical expression of love between my parents was never anything more than a peck on the cheek when my father came home from his travels. The show of love was never openly expressed between my parents, so how could I expect something from them that I never witnessed them give themselves?

When I was eight years old, we moved to a new home in the suburbs of Oshawa. Stephen was now in grade 5, I in grade 4, and Philip and Alison were at home with Mom. This new home that we lived in as a family would soon become a house of grief that would haunt me for many years to come.

CHAPTER 2

At first, the new school and new home were very uncomfortable and foreign to me but I very quickly adapted to my new surroundings. I soon had lots of fun and friends and was excelling academically in school. My drive to be the best powered by my ego was running the show! In being the best, I had to be the center of attention in whatever I did because wasn't that what naturally happened with the best? Academically, I was solid as an oak, but when it came to team sports, this wasn't the case. Hitting the home run, scoring the winning goal, or making the "A" team wasn't a reality for me. I soon accepted the fact that those kinds of activities were not my forte and that I was meant to excel through the power of my brain.

Now, I wasn't the only one to realize my academic excellence. Stephen, who was now in grade 5, was more of a social person than a thinker like me. Stephen also realized his power over me, which was roughhousing and threats. Since I was so smart, maybe I would do his math homework which is a subject Stephen did not excel in. In the event I said no, the consequences would be a beating on my part. At first I said no many times, and as a result, Stephen would rough me up without leaving visual signs like a black eye or bloody lip.

But there's more. If I were to tell our parents, I would not only be branded as a tattletale, and nobody wants to be referred to as a snitch, but Stephen would tell our father that I was still curious about my penis. So here I am again in this fear mode. We were taught that fighting, even self-defense, was unholy and that we should turn the other cheek. Every time I turn the other cheek, I would be smacked on the other side of the head. If Dad caught wind of my sexual exploration, I'd first lose my penis by a butcher knife, then God would send me to Hell. What kind of sick God was this that would allow me, one of his children, to have the tar beat out of me, my penis cut off, and then go to Hell? Needless to say, I did Stephen's homework. But it doesn't stop there.

Stephen had some friends in school who were academically challenged, who he soon informed of his arrangement with me. One person in particular, Rick, followed up to his own benefit. Rick only knew that violence would do the trick and soon approached me.

Rick was the biggest and meanest kid in our school. He was the typical school bully who gained pleasure in seeing others suffer. Here was the deal - I do Rick's math homework, or he would make my life miserable. I already knew what pain felt like from a solid thrashing, and Rick was twice the size of Stephen. This was a no brainer. So now, on top of my own math homework, I had that of two older kids to add to the workload, and they're both in a higher grade than me. I was really beginning to hate my life, and I was only 8 years old! Where was the pleasure or justice in this world of mine? I wasn't allowed to speak or physically defend myself. I wasn't allowed to touch my own body. Open adoration or the mention of money was shunned upon, and I wasn't worthy of affection! Even death had its consequences because if I wasn't perfect from now until death, God was sending me to burn in Hell. As far as I was concerned, I was already in Hell, so why bother? My only question was, "Is this what the rest of my life is going to be like?"

Like other boys, I was becoming more attracted to the opposite sex. Girls were this, and girls were that, but girls still appealed to me very much. There was another boy in our class named Steve who was experiencing the same growth and feelings as I was. Steve and I became good buddies and were soon exceling in everything we did. We both had our eyes on separate girls in our class, and they so happened to be friends. I actually liked two girls – Rhonda was my first "puppy love" (though she didn't notice me) and Dianne who made gestures that she did like me. This was more than convenient for us for obvious reasons. Nothing physical happened between any of us from grade 4 through grade 5, then into grade six. Being a small school, we were always in the same class together. The extent of our desires never went beyond playing around, teasing, and bit of daunting now and then until we hit grade six.

Grade six was a huge relief for me because grade seven and up meant going to a different school. Stephen and Rick were now out of my face, which brought me great relief. My friend Steve and I were now kings of the school and flaunted it proudly. Steve and I weren't bullies because we knew what it was like to be on the receiving end of a handful of knuckles. We helped each other with homework, played together, and even experienced our first kiss together with the two girls we had a shining for since grade four.

On the athletic side, I still wasn't a superstar in hockey, baseball or soccer, but I sure excelled in track and field as well as flag football. The years of running and jumping to escape the beatings sure paid off big time! I was now experiencing success not only on the academic side but on the physical side as well. I joined the flag football team as a wide receiver, with my buddy Steve on the far side. Because I was a strong runner and knew how to catch a ball and run for my life, I scored many touchdowns which aided in our triumph as undefeated in our district. We even had cheerleaders! The girls would form two parallel lines and we would come running down between the lines just like the pros did. This definitely made me feel like a somebody! The school loved me, the fans loved me, and the cheerleaders loved me! My confidence was high, and nothing could stop me.

This gift of running and jumping, acquired by running for my life, was excellent training for track and field. I qualified to represent our school in the 100-meter, 200-meter, 400-meter relay, high jump, and long jump. Every event we went to, we walked away with ribbons. Myself and our team weren't the best in everything, but we always came home with souvenirs of the day's event. It was awesome to hear the students and parents cheering us on from the bleachers as we bolted our way to victory!

With my father away on business most of the time, he was never available to watch me do my thing, and I accepted that because the money to afford this life had to come from somewhere. Of all the events and football games, I distinctly remember my mother coming to one track event. I felt as though my parents didn't love me because of the lack of attention I received doing the things I loved and excelled at. So, I kept up the athletics and my school grades but turned my focus back to making money. I believe since this was my father's focus, if I worked to be more like him I would win more of his attention and affection.

My entrepreneurial skills came into force, and I started making money again. I took on a daily paper route and did substitute work for another route, as well as my lawn mowing business. I had five customers at $5 per week from the business, which carried on into snow removal during the winter months. I soon branched out to do other jobs such as painting, yardwork, and washing cars. I now had money coming in from multiple income streams and figured I had won the game. Nothing had changed with regards to spending the money however - it left my hands as quickly as I could bring it in.

CHAPTER 3

When I was 11 going on 12, I gratefully accepted a job from one of the neighborhood kids named Allen. During Spring Break of 1975, which fell on Easter that year, Allen had proposed to purchase from me a certain type of rock that could only be found along the railway lines. Somehow, these little blue stones about the size of a marble were produced by passing trains. Where and how they came to be, I didn't have a clue, but it was a paying venture. The contract was I would provide a "Crown Royal" velvet bag (you know, the one) full of this slingshot ammunition and I would receive $2. This 11-year-old businessman was prospering and loving every minute of it.

Early that Good Friday morning, I made my plans to venture off to the railway line a mile or so away, a place I had been several times in the past and was familiar with, including the blue stones. I had packed snacks and such the evening before, as well as my pocket knife stowed away in my backpack. Just prior to heading out the door, my mother informed me that I was to watch over Philip, who was now just going on 7 years old. Had Mom known of my plans, there's no way that she would have approved of either of us going there. Taking Philip aside, I explained what I was doing, where I was going, and that if he promised to keep it a secret from Mom and Dad, I would split the money with him 50/50. Philip agreed to join me on this outing and off we went.

The railroad was about 2 miles away, but taking the known shortcuts got us there very quickly. To get up to the track bed, we had to climb a steep embankment that would put us on the outgoing side of the railway. We had followed a local creek, which was now flooded from the melting winter snow and runoff, from our house right to the train tracks, with the raging creek continuing on under the trestle and out to Lake Ontario. We were on the east side of the creek and decided this was the best place to start.

The climb up the tracks was probably 40 feet or so, with the trestle on our right separating us from the other side. Once on top, off we marched off prospecting our goldmine.

After some time of hiking and finding only a dozen or so of these blue stones, I came to several conclusions. Obviously, there weren't many to be found, which meant this would take longer than I had expected. Also, since this would be more work than I thought, I should be charging more for the ones we did find. Lastly, I was tired of walking in this direction, so we decided to head in the other direction. Along the way, we found a few that we had missed during our first pass, but it still didn't amount to much. Before long, Philip and I were back where we started - the trestle.

When we are born into this world, it is a fact that we come with two fears, and all other fears are programmed into our reality. These two fears are of loud noises and falling. By age 11, I was afraid of my brother, violence, my sexuality, heights, falling, and God. Standing at the first railway tie on the trestle, my fear of falling off the trestle was beginning to surface. Needless to say, so was Philip's. I reassured Philip that everything would be fine and that we were sure to find more stones on the other side of the trestle. Besides, the length of the trestle was only 50 feet or so and we'd be on the other side and no time. The other option to get to the other side was to climb down the embankment, walk back several hundred yards to the nearby road, cross over that bridge, then walk back to the embankment and climb up the other side. This seemed like way too much work so over the trestle, we proceeded.

Since we were both afraid of what we were doing, we moved very slowly. The railway ties were several inches apart, a space larger than my foot. Through the gap, we could see only the spring-flooded creek below that was laden with sheets of ice, branches, and debris. I thought that if we fell from the trestle, we would certainly drown and be flushed into the lake. It's funny how the mind can expand and develop thoughts that are crippling.

With eyes glued straight down, ensuring every step was landing on something solid, we inched our way along. All of a sudden, we heard a whistle off in the distance. The track on the other side of the trestle curved away to the left, concealing any possible view of what was ahead. Philip and I stopped dead in our tracks so we could focus on what was ahead and not below. The whistle sounded again, this time much louder. The iron track beneath our feet began to rattle and shake as fear welled up from within us. Again, the whistle sounded louder than before but there was no end to the whistle this time because there it was!!!!

Frozen solid with terror, unable to move, Philip and I stared at the locomotive heading straight for us!! I'm not sure how long we stood there, but it seemed like an eternity. Scrounging up the nerve and strength to move, I turned and faced Philip, shrieking, "Run, Philip run!!" Tears and terror, terror and tears ....

Whistle howling, tracks shaking, and flooded creek below were all there, right there and then. Scrambling, screaming, crying with terror, I leapt off to the right just as the train screeched by, rolling head over heels, ass over tea kettle down the embankment, ending with a solid 'thud' on the creek bank as the train continued by.

"Philip where are you?!? Philip!!"

Succumbed with terror I scrambled around to the other side, searching desperately for Philip, but he was nowhere to be found. "God, where is he?" God did not reply.

Just then, a hand grabbed me by the shoulder from behind, and I was sure it was Philip. I turned around to see an adult standing there with tears in her eyes. She was a local resident who saw everything from her home and raced down to help. I had gone into shock from the terror of what had happened. The sobbing witness walked me by the trembling hand up to her house, called the authorities, and then called my parents.

Everyone was soon there picking up the pieces of the tragedy. The area was swarming with police, firemen, ambulance attendants, neighbors, media and ..... my father. When Dad saw me we fell into each other's arms in relief.

"Dad I'm sorry ... Dad I'm so sorry ..." was all I could muster up.

Dad asked that someone take me home to Mom while he stayed behind at the accident. I never saw Philip anywhere, either dead or alive. People were everywhere, and all that could be heard amongst the crying were sirens. Whoever it was that drove me home that day told Mom what had happened, and then Mom asked me to go to the neighbor's house to get an adult to watch over my younger sister, Alison, and I. My tremendous grief over the accident now turned to panic as I began to take on the blame and guilt for leading Philip to a place of death where he shouldn't have been in the first place. Afterall, "I am the older brother and should know better."

Shortly thereafter, I found myself sitting in the back of a car with Stephen, maybe ours, out front of the emergency entrance to the hospital. Stephen wasn't sure what was going on but was sure to ask, "What have you done now, Kevin?" This day was about to get even worse.

Mom had disappeared inside the hospital with my father while Stephen and I sat impatiently waiting. Leering down the hallway, I saw Mom and Dad speaking with our minister and it was then that I knew Philip was dead. Stephen also now knew that Philip had died, and so he turned his grief and anger on me. First, the verbal abuse of guilt, then right into the physical abuse. I don't remember if he let up because someone saw what was happening or whether he saw Mom and Dad coming our way. Either way, the beating stopped. Our parents emerged from the hospital, embraced Stephen and I, and told us that Philip had passed. We six were now five and we five were about to start a life of tremendous grief, loss and agony.

Our home was now just a house and was full of friends and relatives gathered together to mourn the loss of our beloved Philip. I had hidden myself within the walls of our house to escape any attention and "be unseen and not heard", including no tears ("big boys don't cry", you know) by any adults. In my mind, if Stephen thought this was my fault surely someone else did as well.

I didn't sleep or eat much during the next few days because of the fear and grief I was experiencing. At night when I closed my eyes, all I saw and heard was the train. People were constantly dropping by with groceries and flowers but they were no replacement for Philip. The only way I felt safe was to disappear into the basement or hide outside, quiet and away from everyone. "Out of sight, out of mind" where I could cause no more trouble or trauma. I couldn't even cry out loud for fear of being bad.

The funeral service was several days later and held at the same place Dad once worked years ago. As I sat across from the coffin leering at Philip's motionless pale body, not a single tear came to my eye. Many people came and went and most stopped to console me. "How are you doing Kevin? Are you OK?" they'd ask. In my little mind, I answered quietly, "How the fuck do you think I'm doing?" For the most part I was speechless and simply nodded a yes or no. After the eulogy, Mom, Dad, Stephen and I stood before the open casket in total despair. Again, no tears came to my eyes. In my mind, I pleaded for forgiveness from Philip and God but heard no reply.

The burial was in a small cemetery in a nearby town called Hampton. The four of us and the minister crowded around the desolate black hole that was to be Philip's new home. With the casket slightly raised above the grave, the minister went about his business sending Philip off to a place we were told was Heaven. The minister and I were the only two not in tears as the casket was lowered to the depths below. This was the hardest goodbye I would ever experience.

As the black blanket of soil was placed back to where it belonged, the words "ashes to ashes dust to dust" followed and filled my consciousness. This was the last time I would ever see Philip's joyous face… or so I thought.

Over the years that followed, I would frequent this little cemetery in rural Hampton, ON. At first, I couldn't bring myself to pass beyond the rusty iron gate that housed the bodies within but as time passed, I would gather up the courage to sit at Philip's side for various lengths of time crying, apologizing, begging to die too, or just sit in silence. There was no easy way of knowing what the future held for me, but I was sure of where I would end up. The commandment "Thou shalt not kill" haunted me as there was a truth that lurked within me of what really happened that tragic day when Philip's life was taken. Many times I asked God why he took Philip and not me. I pleaded with God to turn back time and reverse the loss but to no avail. Had God abandoned me? If he was so powerful why couldn't he do this one thing? My so-called faith was dissolving and with it my self-worth.

The coroner's inquest was held in a local courtroom sometime later with all in attendance - family, police, train conductor, witnesses, ambulance attendants, and someone who I perceived to be a judge. As I was called to take the stand, the entire event was flashing before my eyes and all I could hear was the shrieking sound of the train's whistle. The train, the whistle, the paralysis, and Philip's face were all here within my visual touch. I was sworn to tell the truth with my hand on the Bible and then took a seat. I felt that I was on trial and this was "Judgement Day", so I avoided eye contact as much as possible.

"Kevin, in your own words please describe what happened March 31st, Good Friday, when you and Philip were on the railway tracks."

It was all there again, every whistle and every brake screech from the train. When I got to the part about turning to run, something happened inside me. I knew exactly what happened but did anyone else? With a dry gulp swallow, "Philip fell and I tried to help him up but the train was too close so I jumped." I felt nauseous while feeling safe. I lied on the stand that day which created a soul-crushing secret I would bear as my cross from the tender age of 11.

I knew exactly what really happened and so did God. This one lie, which I thought would save my ass, haunted me every second of every minute. By age 12, I was sure God had abandoned me or didn't exist. I often wondered how Hell could be any worse than the life I was already living. Every action has an equal or opposite reaction and this one lie, this one action, would cause a chain of events that would spiral me downwards to a pit of despair much darker than any fathomable Hell I or anyone else could imagine.

CHAPTER 4

The last three months of grade six passed by very slowly. I anxiously awaited the summer months because it meant disassociating myself from the cruelty of some of the kids I went to school with. When I walked through the halls of that small school, conversations and laughter would turn to silence and fingers would point at me like I was something evil or something wrong with me. Some kids would openly make jokes about the accident, calling me "murderer", and others would avoid me completely. Going to school was a nightmare at times. One day I even drank a glass of vinegar to make myself sick so I would not have to go to school. Children can be so cruel.

Before the end of the school year, I started receiving prank phone calls. These calls were more than pranks, they were sick. At first a young voice on the other end of the line would ask for Philip. Then the caller would start asking why I took Philip there in the first place. Finally the caller would accuse me of things such as murder. The voice would never say who they were, but I did recognize the voice. After numerous calls of this nature, I stopped answering the phone all together. The calls soon stopped after that. I never confronted the caller at school, nor have I ever told anyone including my parents about these sick phone calls.

Stephen and I shared a room on the upper floor beside Mom and Dad's room, and Philip's room was down the hall to the left, and Alison's to the right. Of course we had bunkbeds, Stephen claimed the top leaving me the bottom. Good or bad, I don't know, but I do know that every time I closed my eyes either Philip's face came flashing towards me with a terrified look or the massive iron horse with smoke billowing from the stack and steam pressuring out of the whistle as it released the alarm of danger.

I fucking hated it and I was mortified prior to bedtime. Dad, being the handy man that he was, (it's likely where I got some of my skills) built us a study station beneath the window that looked out over the neighboring yards. We each had a desk to work at, Stephen to the left and I on the right, and a dresser built into the middle. I loved my workstation above and beyond its use for homework, but, for the other creative activities I was engaged in.

One Christmas I received a "high tech" radio (well, high tech for the 70's) that functioned as an AM/FM receiver, but also as a Citizen Band radio of sorts. It was really fascinating to listen to voices from faraway places, like living in a Sci-Fi world. My young malleable mind didn't really understand the science and mechanics behind the radio but I did have one primary desire of this radio – to speak with Philip in Heaven. During the quiet and alone fleeting moments, I would scan the airways calling out, "This is Kevin Hanna and I am looking for my little brother Philip. Philip, if you're out there, please speak to me. I am so sorry…". The request always ended the same – no Philip and me sobbing alone in the solitude of my bedroom.

For quite some time, how long I do not recall, I would watch Mom or Dad or both enter into Philip's empty bedroom, close the door and remain there for varying periods. When this happened, I would always leave the house because I believed that when they came out from this crypt of a room, they would be in deep remorse and if I was present, I would be punished. The devastation I lived through was so bad that I could not even walk to that end of the upper floor, could not touch the door handle where Philip once lived or even visit Alison in her bedroom. Going up the stairs to the second floor was an absolute chore as the landing was almost directly across from Philip's room, but going down the stairs was easy because I ran as fast as I could in avoidance.

As I write of these happenings, my heart feels the younger version of me and my inner eyesight vividly witnesses this little boy petrified with fear struggling to live an even quasi-normal childhood. "I love you and cherish you, little Kevin, and this older you is here to hold you and keep you safe. I am always here for you…."

Ok, on with the story. My parents had decided that Stephen and I were at the age that we each required our own room, also because we kept them up at night because of our "disagreements", so one of us would be moving down the hall. I prayed to a God I didn't even believe existed that it would not be me. I can only imagine, now later in my years, the turmoil my parents faced in making this decision because deep down it meant letting go of Philip. The crypt of memories would now transform into a living space and hopefully it would not be mine.

Mom took her time painting and transforming the room into something that would reflect a little boy's room, like denim-fashioned wallpaper and wood shelving. We had an "old as dirt" dresser with a pivoting mirror on top that Mom painted and placed against the wall, and why she chose the off-colored shade of what I thought was pink, I don't know. She even placed a new desk for studies across from the single bed – Philip's bed.

They got Stephen and I together and made their announcement, "Kevin, you will be moving down the hall."

"Seriously?? Are you fucking kidding me? Aren't I traumatized enough? Is this your punishment for me?", I thought quietly to myself. My belongings were packed up and moved without question nor hesitation by my mother, and down the hall I went. Sleep the first night? Are you kidding? I don't recall sleeping through the night EVER while inhabiting that room. Dreams were more vivid and intense because I was truly alone. The only escape was staying awake when I could. Mourning or running into my parents' room was not allowed because "Big boys don't cry", and I do recall the infrequent times I did come begging to my folks that I sleep with them because of the nightmares, but the allowance was very short-lived; when I had calmed down, one of them would escort me back to the room and confirm that this room is now mine and I would have to get comfortable with the decision. Brutal punishment had been established with or without my consent.

In order to make a shift from terror to at least some version of calm, I looked for reasons to appreciate the new room, reasons that were enough to keep me distracted from feeling intense shame, guilt and fear. For starters, I was alone which meant no need to hide my activities and "goings on", starting with adolescent sexual exploration (sounds better than any of the alternatives). "Out of site out of mind" meant no worries about the upper bunk peaking down and embarrassing me. Now, this didn't mean that every time I was alone in the room that I was "exploring", but when the occasion arose, no pun intended, I did have a safe place.

Secondly, pretending any version of my death and resurrection could be more physically animated because there was no one there, except maybe God if he existed. Also, I could utilize my space-age radio scanning the airwaves for Philip without interruption.

Then of course, it was my room which meant that every corner and every wall I could adorn with what was important to me, like my fishing rods and gear, my throwing knife and rock collections as well as any other treasures I had discovered during my adventures into the naked wilderness in our area. Fishing meant tranquility and peace to me. I would escape for hours on end without any care of actually catching a fish. Anything that would take me away from the lie I was living. I had several rods, nets, vest and other gear hanging around my new room that helped me take my mind off Philip.

Wilderness, to me, meant anywhere with a forest and creeks; these were always my sacred places, the places I had and have always had to this day, an indescribable spiritual connection with.

I didn't know the word suicide, but I knew I wanted to die. During the sleepless nights, I would lay in bed and hold my breath thinking that if I did it long enough, I would die. Obviously, this didn't work, but hey, I was a kid so how could I know. Recognizing these failed attempts, I recalled the medicine cabinet that hung above the sink in the bathroom. You know the kind – opening mirrored doors either side, Mom's side and Dad's side. If there's medicine in there then I could consume a bunch of pills and surely that would kill me.

Anything and everything went down the gullet, but taking only enough that my parents wouldn't notice the shortage. Pills of varying colors, coated and uncoated, "horrible when dissolved" pills – if it was in there, I was taking it. Then I would lay in bed and wait …. and wait … and wait. Nothing happened.

I wasn't a fan of physical pain and I didn't have the nerve to cut myself and Dad had disposed of his hunting rifle years ago, so I temporarily put the suicide thoughts aside, and turned my focus to dreaming. Bare in mind, I am 12 years of age; a child, a little boy like your son, or nephew or grandson – 12.

Lying in bed at night I would dream that I was lying in my coffin, casket lid open revealing my breathless body dressed in my finest Sunday School outfit. With hands cupped at the waist, I became the dead "Kevin Arthur James Hanna, son of Llyod Douglas and Elizabeth Cora Hanna." The stage was complete with attendees, which were few in numbers, creepy funeral organ music and the room was filled with the aroma of floral arrangements. Then the minister would begin his eulogy.

As the ceremony came to its conclusion and the family and guests passed by one by one to share their final goodbyes, my little-boy-body motionless and clammy, my stomach would begin to ever so slightly rise and fall with breath. My father, being the last to say goodbye, a solitary tear in his eye, reached across to grip the lid of the casket which would be the beginning of the end of my existence as he hesitantly closed the door to my final home.

Then in a sudden burst of Divine Intervention, my tiny lungs would hysterically gasp for air, my eyes shot open wider than they had ever been and my right hand would reach out to clench the fabric of my father's "mourning black" suit jacket.

"He's alive! Kevin is alive!!

Immediately reaching down with both arms, my father would sweep me up into his loving arms, tears of tremendous joy streaming from his reddened eyes, and declaring to God, "Thank you, Father, thank you for giving my boy back to me!!"

And at the finale of this consciously created dream, I would have the grandest of smiles and heartfelt tears because at the end of the dream, everyone loved me.

Looking back at this, recalling the peril that crippled not only my body but my very soul and existence, I close my eyes and envision standing beside this younger version of myself whispering in his ears, "I love you, Kevin, and I am always here for you. You are safe now to live in peace. I love you." With a deep belly breath, I give myself and little me a hug.

With school out and summer in, life took on a new look and feel. I had a new best friend, a classmate named Michael and we did everything together. All the things little boys do had Michael and I written all over them. We were inseparable. We hiked, camped and fished, played sports, made forts and fires, and laughed. I began to feel at ease as I buried my secret deep within me. I still had nightmares of trains and death, but my daytime reality was bearable. Stephen and I still had our moments, but life was tolerable.

I thought I had put the tragedy behind me and was well on my way to recovery until one night something happened before going to sleep. Now boys will be boys which means we can be mischievous. Michael and I had raised some stink recently by accidentally setting a nearby field on fire. Actually, it was our fort that caught on fire and took to the surrounding grass. Anyway, I was lying in bed just thinking to myself when my Mom poked her head through the door. She was certainly angry about something, but I wasn't sure what. The next thing I heard was her saying, "You're getting away with murder, Kevin!".

Today I know this is simply a phrase which means you're doing things wrong and getting away with it, but at that very moment, I took this literally and personally. Mom closed the door and stormed off.

I didn't sleep at all that night. As far as I knew, Mom thought I murdered Philip, then my mind kicked in with expanded thoughts that she didn't love me, she didn't like me, she didn't want me and she wished it was me that was dead that day. What I thought had subsided was right back in my face but worse. Whether or not my mother remembers this or believes it happened is irrelevant. I heard it and had branded it into my memory along with all the other garbage I was going to Purgatory for.

Now in grade seven, I had a new school with new friends. Grade 7 at that time was one of the toughest grades to pass. Stephen realized this because he had to repeat grade 7, this time with me in the same grade. I often wondered if he failed because I wasn't there to do his homework. It didn't matter to me, because at least we were in different classrooms.

Once again I put my head to work and excelled academically. I still had my paper route, lawn and snow removal businesses as well as other odd jobs. Track and Field were still strong in my veins even though we won less awards. As for hockey, we were the best. We never lost a game in any of the leagues we challenged. Our coach, Mr. Jags, was awesome. He was strict and disciplined but it paid off. We had early morning practices at 6:00 AM twice a week and games once or twice a week as well. I wasn't a goal scorer, but I was a strong aggressive player. Offense or defense didn't matter what line I played because I was always in the midst of the action (unless I was the one with the puck). I loved checking my opponent because it allowed me to release some of the pent-up aggression. I was part of something, a team, which was the best of the best and I loved it.

By now my father was close to the top of the proverbial corporate ladder, which meant most of his time away from home. When early morning practices were on the other side of town, Dad would drop me off on the way to work and I'd catch a ride home with Mike's mom or dad. My father saw some games but not many. For the most part, I'd go to games with Michael and his folks, especially his mother Myrna. After the games, Myrna would always buy us a pop and tell us how wonderful we were. I grew very attached to Myrna because she was giving me a kind of affection that was lacking in my life. Warm hugs, a kiss on the cheek, a cold pop and a compliment went along way with me, and these were offered regardless of my performance on the ice.

That year I scored very few goals, less than 10 actually but I was still a strong player. When I did score a goal, however, I was sure to cut out the bulletin from the sports section of the local newspaper and since I delivered the paper, it was readily available. These I would then pass along to my father with hopes of getting some edification and attention from him. These were some of my greatest souvenirs which I would proudly show off. To this day, my mother still has a trunk of souvenirs I left behind, and on the rare occasion of a visit, I would reminisce of these glorious moments as I rifled through the paraphernalia within the trunk.

My hockey hero was Lanny McDonald of the Toronto Maple Leafs because we played the same position and he had a powerful wrist shot. Mr. Jags wouldn't allow slapshots unless completely necessary, so building a wicked wrist shot was what would score the goals. The best game I played was when I scored two goals in the same game. Both goals were from just inside the blue line along the right boards and were wrist shots that bulleted by the goalie's glove hand shoulder! He didn't have a chance of stopping those babies. We won that game because of those goals and I was the hero for the day. It was upsetting that neither of my parents were there to see me but Myrna was there to congratulate me and my game-winning goals!

All of my equipment was either borrowed or secondhand which meant it didn't fit me or was broken. One day, Mr. Jags dropped by to visit my mother. This call was not to chit chat but to voice his concern that my equipment was less than acceptable, and I could be injured because of it. Nearly everything was too small and should be replaced with up-to-date gear. Mr. Jags then declared that without proper safe equipment, I would be benched and allowed only to be a spectator. I could feel Mom cringe about spending money on hockey gear but I soon had new gloves, pants, shin pads, elbow pads, shoulder pads and skates. It wasn't all brand new but at least it fit. I also had a new helmet soon afterwards. I was the only player in the entire league with a Spalding Helmet which made me feel goofy. This thing looked like something from a sci-fi movie, but hey, at least I was protected and allowed to play.

My hormones were in mass production now and girls took on a whole new meaning to me. Kim was the apple of my eye, but Heather, Linda and Darla were the girls with the breasts. We would meet in the park and swing together as many kids did. The girls would sit on the swing and then let me sit on their lap with my hands up their shirt and fondle their breasts which was truly exciting for me, so much so that sometimes I even ejaculated in my shorts. The more I was allowed to fondle, the more I wanted it, and so did they. We never went beyond kissing and feeling but I didn't care because I was getting action and lots of it. This show of affection from girls was more than just sexual for me. I felt a sense of love from the opposite sex that was somehow filling the maternal void in my heart. My confidence grew because of this and so did my need for physical love. What was once two girls soon became four girls. I subdued my guilt and grief once again and gloried in the things I was excelling at, especially girls and their breasts.

Our family life was still quite shaken, which created walls and barriers between all of us. What warmth once existed was dissolving rapidly. We still had our family outings, like camping or going for ice cream after church, but it wasn't the same.

Summer weekends typically were spent on the boat out at Lake Scugog. Dad, Stephen, myself and sometimes a friend would head out Friday night, then Mom, Alison and others would join us the next day for some fun in the sun. That spring I had seen the movie "Jaws", a tale of a Great White Shark that eats swimmers whole. I had countless nightmares for weeks on end after that on top of the nightmares I already had about Philip and the train. Anyway, one weekend while swimming out at the lake, something started to pull at my leg from the depths below. The tugs became stronger and I started to go under. Panic struck me as the thought of Jaws crossed the video screen of my mind; I was drowning while being eaten alive at the same time! All of a sudden everything stopped and from the depths below up popped a familiar head. Stephen floated before me howling with laughter as he splashed the muddied water at me while chanting that familiar soundtrack from the movie when you know Jaws is coming. Stephen knew I was having nightmares about sharks because we saw the movie together and I expressed my dream to him the following day. Swimming in deep dark waters became my newest phobia. To this day I still avoid entering waters where I cannot see the bottom.

Summer ended and we were back in school for our last year of Middle School. My ego brought me everything that year - good grades, money, girls, and physical attention. I joined the Drama

Club and won the lead role in several productions. No matter how hard I pushed myself there was still something lacking from my life. Was it love and attention or was it honesty? Better yet, was God missing from my life? Through past conditioning, my life was one big sin and God would punish me for it. Was my life the actual punishment God rendered? Approval in love was all I wanted, which is why I strived so hard to impress those around me. This tactic brought very little success and even further diminished my self-worth. Graduation came and went, and summer was here again.

CHAPTER 5

Dad had finished the work on the houseboat early that year, so the plan was to take an extended vacation through the Trent Canal System. This was so much fun passing through the lift locks, fishing, swimming, and meeting new people. We started to resemble a loving family once again.

The Peterborough Lift-lock was the largest lock in the entire canal system, rising several stories in height. The night before arriving at the lock, Stephen and I were fishing side by side at a lock somewhere prior to Peterborough. The only catch I made was the side of Stephen's head. Being so close together, on the outswing of my cast, I had accidentally lodged my hook beneath the skin of Stephen's left temple. Having no car available, my father convinced the lock attendant to drive him to a nearby hospital to remove the hook. Once again, I screwed up, and my punishment was to stay inside the cabin of the boat while we passed through the largest lock on the system, missing out on all the excitement around me. Life really wasn't fair, and I was on the crappy end of the shovel!

Come the end of summer, I would be attending Donovan High School, where I would stay for the next four years. Michael had chosen Eastdale High School as they focused more on trades, arts, and some sciences. This was the beginning of the decline of our camaraderie, as the only time we could hang out was in the evenings. Mind you, the evenings were the best time to raise hell, and I do mean raise hell. We were small-time arsonists (no physical harm done), vandals, thieves, and even broke and entered places, to spout off a few of our shenanigans.

There were a lot of new faces as well as numerous familiar ones from years gone by. Above all else, there were lots of girls. One girl in my Grade Nine Homeroom class, Barb, had an ass so perfectly formed you could bounce a marble off it—and she knew it. As much as I role-played in my mind about her, Barb was out of my league, so staring at her was all my attention would amount to.

My grades remained consistent that year, but sports and track and field interested me very little. My personal cheering section was almost nonexistent, so why bother? I still played hockey and baseball, but only to get me away from home. I enjoyed the camaraderie and the means to release stress, but I never put my all into either of them. I just didn't care anymore about people, life, or myself. I no longer had my paper route, so there was also a huge drop in my income. To compensate for this, I started stealing money from my parents and soon, everyone else and everywhere else I could, regardless of the risk. My father did a lot of traveling to the United States, so I had access to American cash, which paid almost twice as much due to the dollar conversion at the time. I don't know if I became a kleptomaniac because of the instant adrenaline rush, the fear of getting caught, or just to replace my vanished income.

Smoking was what the "cool kids" did, and so did Dad, so it must be good for me, right? So, I took up smoking as well. What I couldn't figure out was why anyone would smoke more than one of those filthy, disgusting things, as I had to fight my way through the first one and every one after that. Before long, I was just as addicted as every other smoker.

At Donovan, we had the option of taking Basic or Advanced curriculum. Naturally, my ego chose the Advanced, as though I had something to prove to everyone. Looking back, I did—self-worth. As long as I did the homework, my grades remained above average. I took no part in scholastic activities because the only reason I was there was that I had to be. School became something I had to do and nothing more.

The new school meant new friends and a new girlfriend, my first girlfriend. Since Mike had opted to go to a trade school down the road, I hung out with a different crowd during the day. This was how I met Anne-Marie. Anne was a year older than me, but we didn't care. Anne also had access to a car, which was an added bonus. Because she was older and had a car, she could buy alcohol—yet another activity the "cool people" did to "fit in." I had never been exposed to alcohol before, outside of a sip of Dad's beer, but now I had been introduced to a new way of escaping reality.

One night, before a school dance, we all headed over to a buddy's house with the goal of getting drunk. I had split a case of beer with a friend, and no sooner had we opened it than I had guzzled half the case within thirty minutes. We stumbled over to the school and discreetly passed through security. The music was loud, and the strobe lights illuminated the gymnasium. I felt a grumbling in my stomach, and the room began to spin. Like a bolt of lightning, I was out the door and into the boys' washroom. I never even made it as far as the first stall when everything blew.

Beer and chunks flew everywhere. I not only ruined my shirt but managed to throw up on another kid as well, which created a new enemy—and one physically bigger than me. Puke was everywhere, including my nostrils.

One of the guys grabbed the rest of the gang, and we split before we could be expelled. The night didn't end there, however. One of the guys had a 40-pounder of vodka stashed away. With no opener for the can of tomato juice, we punctured a hole through the tin top with a rock. The bottle and mix were passed around the circle— taking a gulp of one, then a chug of the other. I didn't merely gulp; I drank it like it was water! Now I was really wasted, along with having bits of broken rock in my mouth.

The next thing I recall was lying in the middle of the road outside the corner store, about a mile or so from where we passed around the alcohol alongside the creek in a wooded area. Eyes barely able to focus, I caught a glimpse of flashing red lights and knew it had to be the police. I was so drunk that I couldn't even pull myself off the road to escape. All of a sudden, I was dragged to my feet and carried through the cemetery across the road and dumped. Everyone took off, leaving me at the top of a rather large hill. Turning to face the store, I saw the police had arrived, which was my cue to run. But how could I run if I couldn't walk? One step over the edge was all it took to send me ass-over-teakettle down the hill and into the creek bed below. I'm not sure how long I laid there in that cold, refreshing water, but the boulder my head slammed into wasn't exactly a great pillow.

I came to my senses and fumbled my way through the dark to our home, which was literally across the creek bed, up the gravel pit bluffs, and around the corner. The lights were still on, and there was an additional car in the driveway. I was a total write-off but figured I could fake my way up to my room. The thought of sleeping it off outside never even occurred to me. I pried open the garage door and fell face-first into the trunk lid of Mom's car. That was all it took to bring my parents to see what was going on.

"Hi, Dad," I gurgled, with a shit-eating drunken grin on my face and blood droplets on my forehead above my eye.

My father lifted me up and carried me upstairs while Mom asked the company, which I recognized as my Aunt Shirley and Uncle Abbe, to leave. I don't recall much else from that evening other than my father sitting over me all night as I slept it off.

The next morning, I was lectured on the abuse of alcohol and grounded indefinitely. I clearly remember my father telling me that the reason he stayed up all night with me was because he was worried I'd have alcohol poisoning. The night before, I had taken my life into my own hands and jeopardized it—but more importantly, I had won the attention of my father. After all those years chasing the pursuit of excellence to gain approval, I realized that what worked best was self-abuse.

The grounding lasted a couple of weeks, and soon I was out partying with my friends again. Every Friday night, Anne-Marie's folks would head out for the night, leaving her in charge of her three younger brothers. Anne-Marie's parents knew we partied but preferred we do it there rather than on the streets of Oshawa. Anne-Marie would provide the booze and location; all we had to do was show up. In this drunken state, I could be anyone I wanted to be. As long as I was intoxicated, there was no pain or grief. At the age of fifteen, I was now accustomed not only to being drunk but to sneaking into the house while my parents slept. Or did they?

Anne-Marie and I were so close that we were inseparable. Anne would let me do anything I wanted with her body, except intercourse. We would sit on the couch together in the family room and watch TV with a blanket pulled up to our waists—unbeknownst to everyone else that my fingers were playing with Anne's vagina. I was so enamored with her that I had a much nicer life there than at my own house. This created a tremendous amount of friction at home because I wasn't participating in any family events, including meals. Why should I? I had more love and attention with Anne-Marie's family than my own.

This relationship with Anne-Marie lasted until the next summer vacation. Anne-Marie and her family took a two-week vacation to Eastern Ontario, leaving me in charge of their home. Those two weeks seemed like an eternity, as Anne never called or wrote to me the entire time. I was so elated the day they returned that I ran all the way to her house to greet her. To my dismay, the first words out of her mouth were, "I'm breaking up with you." Devastation is the only word that comes close to what I was experiencing.

This couldn't be true—we were in love. Anne told me she met someone else during her holiday and that she had even lost her virginity to that person. That was all I needed to hear. Crushed by someone I thought loved me, I hit what seemed to be an all-time low. I didn't eat or sleep for days. I passed endless hours wandering the streets toward her house, wondering why. My despair soon turned to anger and resentment towards Anne-Marie, and then towards women in general. I felt used and abused by all the women in my life and vowed it would never happen again. I closed the door to my heart and threw away any possible notion that love existed. My prime directive was now me and only me.

With summer vacation over and school back in session, I had a totally new outlook on life. All I cared about was keeping up my grades—just enough to maintain passing grades—and sex. I was determined to lose my virginity and have sex with as many girls as possible. With all the girls in our school, this should have been a simple task, I figured. By mid-fall, I had several girls on the line, but never made it with any of them. I was frustrated with this pursuit, but at least I was having fun.

One afternoon, while skipping class, a neighborhood kid asked me if I'd like to go buy some marijuana with him. I'd never smoked pot before and never really wanted to because of all the bad publicity I'd heard, but I decided to go along to see what all the hype was. We met up with an older kid I recognized from some years past and bought several joints from him.

I had been smoking cigarettes for over a year now, so taking a puff from that joint didn't seem like it could be a big deal if I decided to do it. My friend Mike was with us also and wasted no time sparking one up for himself. This is where peer pressure kicked in, and I took a drag for myself. That first inhale almost made me choke to death! It was so gross, I had to do it again and again until I could actually hold it in. Within an hour, all the joints were gone, and my head was spinning. I didn't feel sick, but I was in some kind of euphoria that wasn't real or unreal.

We wandered around for several hours in a daze until the effects wore off. This high was much different from what I experienced with alcohol because at least I had some control and no nasty headache afterward. Later that night, we bought more drugs and smoked every one of them as well. Tobacco was the gateway addiction to "soft narcotics" and an entire world of darkness and crime to follow.

It's a well-known fact that anything is attainable as long as there is a burning desire to go for it. As more focus, attention, and action are put toward a desired outcome, eventually that outcome becomes reality. Addictions work the same way. What starts out as a simple thought creates a direct action. As the frequency of thought increases, so does the frequency of actions. We've now created a habit. Habits can be good or bad, depending on who's judging. In my case, the thought was to escape reality and the lie I was living. The action that resulted was the introduction to sex, drugs, and alcohol. The end result was temporary euphoria, which is what I desired, but the habit created by dependency on those stimulants was a reaction I had not anticipated.

The deeper I fell into this false reality, the dimmer the light of life became. My dependency on stimulants became so strong that nothing else mattered. I had given up all entrepreneurial endeavors and replaced them with stealing, lying, cheating, and "sexual depravities" (according to the Bible). The family structure was totally dysfunctional, so I stayed away from home as much as possible. Athletics were out of the question, as I was my only fan, and my grades dropped dramatically. To receive a graduate diploma, each student required 27 credits over the four years of high school. No spares were given during the first year but could be taken starting in the second year. I had it all down to a tee. I would graduate on schedule with 27 credits and have two spare periods per year for the next three years. Easy, right?

Narcotics exposed me to a whole new world of people and violence. These were the people I thought were my friends. To keep up with my addiction meant I needed to increase my income. I stole money from friends, family, extended family, neighbors, and people I simply didn't know. I pawned stolen articles, broke into houses and school lockers, arena dressing rooms, and even ran fraudulent fundraisers. The addiction was so strong I couldn't escape it. Buying and selling drugs became buying and smoking them, as I was my best customer. Dealers and gangs were after me for late payment as I smoked my way into oblivion. What drugs I couldn't buy, I would steal from other addicts I hung out with. Death threats became a common occurrence, as did paranoia.

My school grades dropped from an "A" average to barely passing. All my teachers knew who I was and why my grades were down. Some teachers even played practical jokes on me in class, like throwing a pencil at me to see if I could catch it. The classes I didn't like, I skipped, knowing that as an Advanced Grade student, all I required was 35% to receive a lower grade credit. I had totally given up on family, God, and more importantly, myself. I hated myself and life so much that I just wanted to disappear without a trace.

One day, on the way to school during my final year, we noticed a crowd gathered along a nearby bridge. Police were everywhere securing the area. Hanging from the bridge was a rope and a bright yellow bag with feet dangling from the bottom. I soon found out that Alex, a fellow troubled junkie, had hung himself that morning. Alex was the dealer we purchased our first joints from. I remember thinking how lucky Alex was because now he didn't have to put up with all the bullshit of living. My biggest concern was whether school would be canceled for the day because of it. How messed up is that?

I lost my virginity that year to Monica and started dating several other girls at the same time. It was simple to weasel my way in with expressions of love, get what I was after, and then dump them. I was a male whore, to say the least. One girl who really liked me, Jolene, asked me to go to the Senior Prom that Spring. Jolene was a vibrant, honest, clean girl who, in my sober days, really appealed to me. I told Jolene I was already going with someone else but thanked her for her offer. In reality, there was no one else, and I had no intention of going, as I didn't want to stand out—not that I had anything to celebrate anyway. What an asshole I had become.

It's important to mention that when Stephen first found out I was using drugs, he made me aware of his disapproval. Within the next year, he was on drugs as well but came by his "honestly." Our folks both knew what was going on and even went as far as to recommend counseling for me.

Our family unit had totally collapsed and fragmented to a point where we weren't even on speaking terms. Our folks' hair turned gray prematurely, and other stress-related health issues also developed. The way I saw it was that they did it to themselves, and if they had loved me all along, this never would have happened. To hell with them and to hell with me was my motto.

CHAPTER 6

Stephen had developed a reliable source for drugs and soon introduced me to his dealer. They were a husband-and-wife team living 20 minutes from our home. At first, Stephen didn't approve of me being at their house because they were his friends. Having such easy access to the drugs I needed resulted in extended periods of time with this couple. I began purchasing small quantities of marijuana on a regular basis with the money I had fraudulently acquired until I had established enough credibility to get larger amounts fronted to me. I would then turn around and sell enough to pay for the drugs and smoke the remainder or smoke it all and steal enough money to cover the debt. Accumulating wealth by selling all the drugs didn't even occur to me, as I was happiest when I was stoned. Hindsight being 20/20, had I stayed with buy and sell only, the profits would have allowed me to purchase my first house before even graduating high school. The dealers and I had become good friends by developing a relationship that was beneficial for both of us.

Grade 12 had come and gone in what seemed to be a blur. Report cards were issued in June, and to my dismay, I had failed by one credit. This meant no diploma and no graduation. The class I had missed was math, which at one time had been my strongest subject. To top it off, I missed the General Math credit by one percentage point. That is, 35% in advanced math was required to achieve a passing grade in the General course. I had attained 34%! I approached Mr. Chung, the math teacher, and pleaded for that 1%. His response was that had I at least come to class, he would have granted my request. He pointed out that I had missed more than half the year of classes. The only way to make up the grade was to either take the class over the next year, go to summer school, or take one semester in another local school. I had screwed myself royally this time. The hardest part was yet to come, as I had to explain the situation to my parents. Mom I could deal with, but my father was someone whom I inwardly looked up to and admired all along but was now afraid of. I felt that I not only let myself down but him as well. How could any father possibly be proud of me now? All my friends and my brother were going to graduate without me that year.

It was a painful experience for the three of us to deal with, but that fall, I enrolled for one semester of Chemistry at an alternate high school. Not that I wanted Chemistry, but there were no available spaces for Grade 12 Math. The course began well, but after several weeks I dropped out. I had one class a day that happened to fall right in the middle of the day. This meant no full-time job or goofing off at all. This mid-day class was cramping my lifestyle, so I quit, which was another disappointment for myself and my parents.

I took on multiple small jobs here and there but had no skills that qualified me for anything outside of general labor at $5 an hour. The new deal was that if I wasn't going to school, I had to work and pay for room and board at $35/week. I think I paid once or twice during the next year because all my money was going towards my addictions.

The tension between myself and my parents turned to anger and spite that year. My life was going absolutely nowhere as I buried myself with alcohol and drugs. I had at least a dozen different jobs that year, and I quit each one. I wanted big-paying jobs handed to me on a silver platter because I felt life owed me that much in compensation for all the crap I had been through. No such luck. I took my parents' advice that those types of jobs could only be had with an education. In the spring of 1982, I enrolled in a summer school math class, which I passed with flying colors and obtained my final credit required for my high school diploma. That same summer, following the same advice, I enrolled at the Community College for a course in Business Management. I wanted to impress my father and be successful just like him, so this must be the way to do it.

My bond with the couple supplying me with drugs had grown very strong, especially with the wife. One evening, while visiting with her while everyone else was gone fishing, she asked me to sit beside her on the couch. She got me high on her stuff, then asked me to kiss her. I was shocked and not quite sure what to do—she was 33 years old. Sex and drugs had become my life, and she assured me her husband would never know. What started out as a kiss developed into full-on carnal sex. We played hard and fast, then slow and deep until we were both exhausted. She was needy, and so was I. That one night of carnage—a night of free drugs and sex with an older woman—was about to send me even deeper into the notorious depths of Hell. What I had perceived as a raw deal in life was now even shittier.

College courses started in September, but I opted to pass again. I was rebelling against society, myself, and especially my father. I admired my father tremendously, but at the same time, I wanted nothing to do with him or to be like him. I did everything possible to sever myself from my father. I had once put him on a pedestal of greatness that consequently made me feel inferior and useless. Deep in my heart, I wanted to shine, to stand out, and make a difference, but this wasn't something members of our family did. "Nose to the grindstone" and "fly under the radar" were our family mottos. In my eyes, I was a loser who didn't deserve love or respect. My father and I didn't seem to have anything in common, and he would never take me in his arms and allow me to finally mourn and confess, so why fight it?

My days were spent walking the streets in search of a quick high, which always took my mind off who I thought I was or who I wanted to become. In the evenings, I would visit my dealers because I knew I would get stoned and drunk for free. On top of that, the wife would give me a ride home in the van and then virtually rape me before dropping me off. This went on for months without a hitch. Her husband had no idea she was getting it elsewhere, or from the 18-year-old boy sitting beside him on the couch, smoking his weed and drinking his beer!

Affections grew strong for the both of us, so our little rendezvouses started happening daily. Gifts of her affection became numerous, like jewelry, money, and drugs. The more she got it, the more she wanted. I was practically living there at this point, though I never spent the night under their roof. The husband, my brother, and I would go fishing and camping regularly, which was a good way to help balance the scales. I figured by spending time with him, he would never find out. One weekend, Stephen, the husband, and

I even went to my father's cottage for the weekend. Obviously, my father never knew about this, or he would never have allowed it. We were wasted for three days straight.

Opening day for Muskellunge, a rather large predatory fish, arrived quickly that spring. We had all planned to take the boat, get high, and win the derby at Lake Scugog. At the last minute, I decided to stay behind and help paint the house with Nancy. Everyone was shocked, but no questions were asked. I simply explained that I had no desire to sit in a boat for 12 hours in the pouring rain. What I didn't say was that I planned to fuck Nancy all day. I helped load the boat, wished everyone luck, and sent them on their way. At last, let the sexual feasting begin!

I waited at least half an hour before jumping all over my experienced sex toy. There wasn't a room in the house we didn't explore. In between romps, we would paint and listen to country music until I was able to get another erection, and then we would go at it again. I was a teenage boy in his glory because I had what most guys my age only dreamed about—tits, ass, and a lot of fucking!

Around 2:00 in the afternoon, still lying in bed drenched in lusty sweat, we heard a vehicle door slam outside the front of the house.

"Fuck! They're home!"

Terror struck us both as we floundered to get dressed before anyone entered the house. I grabbed my clothes, though I couldn't find my socks, and bolted for the bathroom. Screaming and hollering filled the house instantly as the front door swung open. I had no idea where Nancy went, but I was now dressed somewhat presentably and descended the stairs to see what the commotion was all about. My heart was pounding so hard and fast I thought

I was going to upchuck right there and then! This man was over 6' tall, 250 pounds, and covered in tattoos, with a glare that could melt a nail!

Joe just stared at me with suspicious eyes. All was now silent. Did he know?

"What's up? Why all the yelling?" I managed to squeak out like a church mouse.

I was then presented with a fish that had to be 4 feet long, if not longer! "We won the Derby, let's party!" he bellowed.

The fish was a once-in-a-lifetime catch, so eating it was out of the question. We cleaned the guts out, then packed it safely away in the freezer. Now we were going to get into some serious partying.

We drank, popped uppers, and smoked for hours on end. Actually, I had never seen Joe party like this before. My intuition was telling me he knew what was going on. He'd give me a glare of death that would send shivers down my spine. Then he'd grab me in a bear hug and tell me how much he loved me. He paid absolutely no attention to his wife or anyone else there, just me.

"Kevin, I have something to show you. Come upstairs for a minute."

I had no idea what he was up to, but I could not deny his request. I followed Joe upstairs to the master bedroom, and to my surprise, Nancy had made the bed. There on the floor before me were my socks. He didn't notice them, so I picked them up and shoved them into my pants pocket. Fumbling through a jewelry box, he pulled out a bulky chain necklace and turned to face me with it. The necklace was a heavy gold choker that looked like something a gangster would wear, and Joe was certainly the gangster type. He asked me to close my eyes while he placed it around my neck. Once attached, he moved it around my neck a couple of times.

"This choker has an invisible link that connects it. Here's the deal, Kevin: if you can find the link and get it off, it's yours. If you can't get it off… I'm going to kill you."

My heart stopped dead, and beads of sweat were now pouring down my face. I knew that he knew something. His glare was treacherous, and his gold-capped smile terrified me. Very calmly and methodically, I felt each link, looking for some irregularity while maintaining eye contact. Unconsciously, I was praying to a God I doubted even existed for his assistance. I could feel droplets of urine running down my leg. Time stood still for what seemed like an eternity. Was I going to die at the hands of a jealous husband, or would I have a new necklace?

I came to a link on the chain that didn't move like the others, so I put all my remaining strength and prayers of desperation into prying it open. The choker snapped and fell to the floor, and then so did I.

My life was spared for the moment. I could feel the tears welling up inside me, but I forced myself not to cry. He offered me the choker, but I diplomatically declined, saying it "wasn't my style," though the reality was it reminded me of how close I had come to death there in the bedroom. All Joe did was stare at me in silence. Was he going to kill me anyway, I wondered? He let out a booming laugh, grabbed me by the neck, and forced me down the stairs.

Stephen was sitting on the couch, oblivious to what was going on, and Nancy was in her habitual recliner. I popped open a beer and guzzled it without hesitation. Then I rolled a fat joint and smoked the entire thing, not allowing anyone else a hit. My heart slowly descended from my throat back to its place of origin, and I melted back into the couch beside Joe. I had certainly pissed myself, though not visibly to anyone else in the living room.

No sooner said than done, Joe jumped to his feet and tore off his shirt. His upper torso resembled a giant inkblot, as the paleness of his skin had been replaced with multiple tattoos. This man was huge! Hyperventilating, his chest expanded bigger and bigger, and then he threw his glasses on the floor and yelled out, "Are you fucking my wife?"

Aside from the wheezing of his short breaths, you could have heard the ping of a pin hitting the floor. "Be a man for once and do the right thing," I said to myself. Rising to my feet, shoulders back, chest out, chin up, "Yes," I declared. His gigantic fist came thundering down on the glass coffee table, shattering it into a million little crystals.

"Get the fuck out of my house!" he thundered.

I didn't even hesitate to grab my shoes as I bolted out the door. I knew he would be coming to kill me, so I ran full out back to our house. Within minutes, I had several necessities packed and ready to go. Mom and Dad were in the family room downstairs, watching TV, and were oblivious to what was going on or what was about to happen. The phone rang once and only once before I picked up the receiver. It was Nancy.

"Kevin, I'll be there in 15 minutes to pick you up. We've gotta move, NOW! He's coming to kill you!!!" Click—the line went dead.

"Holy shit!! What do I do?" I ran downstairs to confront Mom and Dad.

"I have to leave for a while. Something has happened, but I can't explain. I'll call you in a couple of days. I love you both."

I left no room for questions or explanations. My fear carried me out the front door and into the waiting van. I forced Nancy out of the driver's seat and stomped the gas pedal to the floor. There were no real hiding spots within town, so I drove all night along the back roads of Durham County.

Come sun-up, I had no idea where we were or where we were going. She actually had enough cash for a meal and gas to keep us moving. It wasn't until now that I noticed Nancy showed no signs of physical violence. There were no bruises or cuts, no broken bones. The night before, I was sure someone besides me would receive a thrashing. As it turned out, there was a lot of screaming and crying, but only on his part. Several other things in the house were broken, but he never laid a hand on her. There was someone who did receive the violent end of the stick, however, and that was Stephen. In a fit of rage, Joe had thrown Stephen through the plate glass front door. He wasn't seriously injured, but he did receive the scars that should have been mine.

Nancy and I spent the next two days driving around the back roads of Ontario in an attempt to avoid the wrath of her husband. I had arranged to go home to speak with my folks, who lovingly gave me some money and allowed me to use one of their vehicles. Both of them were in tears, agonizing over the fear of my destruction. Stephen also had a few choice words for me, but more importantly, he told me that Joe had visited my father the day before. His intention was clearly to find me and then kill me. My father had dropped to his hands and knees and begged Joe not to harm me. You must understand that my father is an extremely proud man, so for him to exhibit this act of love for his son was unprecedented. In fact, my father was so fearful of what may happen that he sent my mother and sister to live with my aunt until everything subsided.

Nancy and I knew that Joe would be at work, so we swung by their house and dropped off the van. Their two kids were home from school, so we visited for a very short while. They seemed alright with what was happening because, from my viewpoint, they didn't like their abusive father anyway. Nancy packed up her things, including a bag of 'goodies' for my addiction, and we left.

Nancy couldn't afford to miss any more work, so we found a place to live close to her job. I moved in and started looking for employment myself. It was time for me to be responsible, as I now had a ready-made family. Several weeks later, the kids joined us. Nancy's son was 14, and her daughter was 12. I was young enough to be their older brother!

This was an extremely awkward situation to be in, as I didn't know how to relate to these kids. To one, I was a buddy, and to the other, I was an infatuation. Every time I was left alone with the daughter, she'd hit on me. Obviously, I denied the flirtations, but in doing so, she would tell her mother I was doing some very inappropriate things with her. This was one messed-up situation.

All the money I received from odd jobs went to Nancy for living expenses. It wasn't fair to Joe to deny him access to his kids, so he came around on a regular basis. Joe had no idea I was living there, so every time he visited, I would hide in the dilapidated garage out back. On one of his visits, Joe stayed for three days, so for three days I lived in the damp and dark garage along with a family of rats. I couldn't understand how Nancy could say she loved me yet spend so much time with her estranged husband. Actually, it infuriated me. Whenever I confronted her with my concerns, she simply replied that it was Joe's right to visit, and they were still legally married. What kind of love was this anyway?

The new style of living was now several months old and had not progressed but regressed. Finally, I had enough of this bullshit and phoned my parents, asking if I could come back home. The answer was a conditional 'yes'. I'd find out the conditions when I got home.

I waited for a time when the kids were in school and Nancy was at work before going inside to pack my things. Right in the middle of packing, who should walk in the door but Joe. My heart stopped dead, and so did his. Nothing but silence. Joe calmly walked up to me, threw the rest of my things into a garbage bag, and told me to follow him outside. What was he up to, I wondered. He chucked all my belongings in the car and told me to get in. Were we going to the country for a "ride"? Was he going to kill me? Was he going to maim me? I didn't know, but my guts were on the verge of exploding.

Joe fired up the Cordoba and pulled out of the driveway without a word. Twenty minutes of dead silence passed. I was so scared that my innards let loose, and I shat my pants. To my surprise, he pulled up in front of my parents' house and turned to face me. "Get out of the car, Kevin, and don't ever let me see your face again, or I will kill you next time. And if it's not me, then it may be my brother, Eddie."

That was all I needed to hear to change my opinion about Nancy. I realized that all Nancy was to me was female physical attention and free drugs. Nothing more, nothing less. It was easy to fall out of love with her once I understood this. I never went back after that, even though she continued to call me. To me, she was now like a plague. As it turns out, Joe and Nancy never did get back together, even though I think they were made for each other.

Several months later, Joe figured he would take his aggression out on my family. Now, this is my own speculation, but I believe it to be true. One day, my father received a call from a neighbor who was looking after our cottage near Gooderham in Northern Ontario. Someone had broken in, smashed all the glass, shot holes in the appliances, chopped up the antique dressers, and then poured gasoline over all the beds and furniture. Dad and I raced up to the cottage to meet with the local police to investigate the crime.

The cottage was a write-off. While doing my own investigation, I found a cigarette butt that looked very familiar. It was lying on top of a gasoline-drenched stack of paper. The brand was Medallion Extra Lite, the exact same brand Joe smoked. In fact, he was the only person I knew who smoked them. I figured I had solved the crime, so I informed my dad and the police. It had to be Joe, as far as I was concerned, because all the facts pointed to him. He had a motive, he smoked this brand of cigarette, and he knew exactly where the cottage was. It had to be him.

I'm not sure what happened after that because the case miraculously disappeared. There was no trial, nor was there any evidence that the police contacted Joe. I began to wonder if my father accepted the fact that it was Joe and scratched it off as the debt being settled. I messed up his life, so he messed up my father's life. To this day, I still don't know and don't want to know. It was time to move on.

The conditional "yes" to moving back home seemed pretty straightforward to me. I was to either go back to school or get a job. There were to be no drugs, booze, or partying all night as long as I lived there, and I was to quit smoking. Mom and Dad were extremely adamant about this for obvious reasons. As for me, I wanted to clean up my act anyway, so I agreed.

I started looking for any type of work, which really boiled down to being a laborer of sorts, as I had no other skill sets. I found several casual jobs and soon realized I loved the money so much I didn't need school. This was fine with my folks as long as I continued to work and pay $35 per week for room and board. That was a great deal for me because I was eating $35 worth of groceries every couple of days! The jobs I had all paid minimum wage, which was $5 an hour. No matter how hard I worked or how many hours I put in, it still added up to peanuts. There had to be a better way. I figured that if I quit using drugs and sold them instead, my income would increase dramatically. I knew I had made a promise to my parents, but my paycheck really sucked, and I wasn't about to go back to school. I called up a friend who had connections and arranged my first purchase.

For the first few weeks, everything was great. I wasn't using, and I was making a profit. While counting my profits with a friend, he suggested we celebrate my win, and what better way than to get high? I boldly refused and explained that I had no intention of going back to that lifestyle. The days of violence, deceit, theft, lying, and sex-for-trade were gone, and that's the way it was going to stay. This "friend" agreed that a couple of joints wouldn't make me turn around and that he would make sure of it. All he wanted was to get high on my dime. To settle the matter, I gave him a joint of my finest Columbian. The aroma that filled the air from the smoke that spiraled from the joint brought back memories of "quiet thoughts" and peace. It was enough for my ego to take over and demand a puff.

Oh, it was so good! At the end of that joint, we sparked several more. Very soon, I was in a world of make-believe where nothing mattered. That one event that one afternoon of inebriation, immediately sucked me back into a world of hate and anger. My profits declined, and my debt soared. My health plummeted, and my social and family life disappeared. I was back in the darkness.

For those who have been addicted to drugs, you know as well as I do that when you fall off the wagon, the addiction becomes stronger. Your ego is once again in control, like an alternate personality. No matter how hard you try, your ego slaps you in the face and declares that this is where you belong. It's not long until you actually accept the false belief, and your self-worth is basically nonexistent. This is exactly where I was—over my head in self-pity, guilt, and shame. I was a pathological liar and kleptomaniac. I used and abused everyone that came within my circle of influence. My acting skills were honed so sharply that I could play any part in achieving my goals.

In most cases, I was never discovered as the perpetrator of the crime or act. However, there were those instances where I was found out and reprimanded. My "friends" now consisted entirely of other druggies and women who I could still toy with by trading sex for things I required, like cash or food. I had become a very despicable person, and the worst part was that I realized it.

In Oshawa, my regular stomping ground was the Main Street Bar, a dark and dingy hole in the basement of the Genosh Hotel. Headbangers, hookers, druggies, drunks and musicians were the regular clientele of this establishment. Every weekend featured a new band which drew crowds from all around the city. Some bands went on to stardom, while others remained garage quartets. The crowd was rough and raunchy, not to mention untrustworthy. Using the facilities was like some kind of recon mission right out of a war movie. I always tried to hold my yearnings to piss for as long as possible, and when the time came, I always made sure someone was there to watch my back. Really, this place was a shithole. I even made it a point to sit with my back against the wall so I could see everything coming at me. Paranoid? Maybe, but there were those who really had it in for me, like Joe's younger psychotic brother Eddie who was known to frequent the bar.

Upstairs was the Pink Flamingo Room, a strip bar featuring beauties from around the globe. This was usually the first bar we hit before going downstairs. A few shots and naked breasts were always enough to get us gunned up and cocky for the duration of the evening. Like the saying goes, "Sex, drugs and rock'n'roll!!"

One particular midweek evening, I found myself wandering the streets alone. I was in a lull that kept me contemplating what my options were. I hated my life and who I had become. I had no friends, no family, no money and no ambition. What better place to meet someone I could relate to than the Genosh Hotel. I meandered into the dingy shithole I called home and took a seat. The bar was empty except for a hand full of other losers, probably contemplating the same things I was. I ordered a Budweiser, a "real man's beer" according to the crowd and sunk deeper behind my table.

There was no music or words spoken throughout the bar, no action whatsoever. As I looked around the room, I realized that I had more similarities with these patrons than I'd thought. It dawned on me that I was as much a part of them as they were of me. Ouch!! That really hit home because I despised these people. They were pathetic losers to me which meant I too had become a pathetic loser. Something inside me snapped. This was the first time ever that I could not finish my drink. I packed my leathers and left immediately.

It took me nearly an hour to make the 20 minute walk home. Was it the despair or the midnight rain that slowed me down, or a combination of both? Like so many thousands of times before, I made my way to the rec room in the basement with not so much as a peep. Sitting still as the night, I glared at the pad of paper and pen sitting on the coffee table beside me. My mind was turbulent yet peaceful. My body was tense yet limp. I knew exactly what to write and to whom. It began with "Dear mom and dad..."

By the end of the letter, I had bequeathed all my worldly possessions to those that were still somewhat attached to my life, not that I had much of either, apologized for trauma and drama and sins I had committed. Laying the letter aside, I went to Dad's utility room at the back of the basement and took a bottle of Killex Weed Killer from the shelf and returned to the rec room. I poured a tall Tupperware cup of the lethal weapon then sat on the couch. "I'm sorry", I said aloud, then chugged the entire cup without hesitation then laid down to end my life.

Everything was quiet and dark. I could feel my mouth, throat and stomach burning as the poison corroded away the flesh. Behind closed eyelids, there was no light or tunnel just darkness. Black is black but this darkness was getting blacker and deeper. I felt myself descending like a leaf falling from a tree in the Fall. Was I descending into the depths of the biblical Hell? I had no recollection of time or space. I didn't even know if I was dead or alive until a tiny voice, my voice, muttered inside, "I don't want to die.."

My eyes flicked open and tears flooded my heart. I found myself being "pushed" off the couch onto the floor with a thud. This same force or strength or whatever it was, dragged my sorry ass on hands and knees up two flights of stairs and into my parents' bedroom then dropped me on the end of the bed. I knew my parents were now awake because I recall hearing my dad say, "What the...?" The only word I could muster up was "Suicide..."

I was in and out of consciousness from that point on. I recall being crumpled up on the bathroom floor, head in the toilet and my father's finger down my throat.

I recall looking up to see a strange man in a white shirt hovering over me.

I recall laying on a table and having something forced down my throat then soon after sitting upright, yelling at the top of my lungs, "Get this fucking shit out of me!!", then darkness.

Sometime later, was it an hour or day or several days, I don't know, I opened my eyes once more. The darkness was now fading to a blur and in the blur I recognized two faces hovering over me. As my focus came to a point of recognition, the figures I saw above me were my mother and our minister, Reverand Turner. A stray look at my body revealed that there were wires and tubes attached to me that connected my being to several electronic gadgets and liquid filled bags. The only thought that came to mind was I was dying. Why else would the minister be here? My head hit the pillow, the strength that held my eyes open disappeared, and I slipped back into darkness.

During the following days, how many I'm not sure, I was neither here nor there. I couldn't tell if I was dead or alive, dreaming or awake, in Heaven or in Hell. Wherever I was, my mother's face was always before me. Sometimes she was weeping, other times it seemed as though she was praying. Whatever the case, mom was inherently there with me the whole time.

After several days had passed, I realized I was alive and that I was hospitalized. I now found myself questioning my actions and thinking that somehow I had screwed up again. I couldn't even get suicide right. I had been moved from Intensive Care to a common room in "G-Ward", or the Psychiatric Ward. I was ashamed and deeply embarrassed to be there but as I began to notice the other patients with me, it dawned on me that these people were not your typical psychos or loonies we commonly see promoted in the movies. These people were sane and had emotional troubles just like me. This realization truly eased my mind.

I was granted visiting rights but wasn't permitted to leave the ward. Every day one or both of my parents came to see me. Even my brother Stephen had made an appearance. We laughed and cried during these visits and vowed that everything would work out in the end. We all knew my actions were rooted in the death of Philip, though we never really voiced this common knowledge. I was there to get better and that was it. I also had visits from several other friends and family during this stay which showed me that there were others out there that truly cared for me. I was embarrassed when these visitors first entered the room but was soon immersed in love as each shared their compassion with me. It is so true that one doesn't know their true friends until tragedy strikes.

My therapy consisted of an assortment of pills taken several times a day along with group discussion sessions. When I questioned the nurse about the necessity for the rainbow of pharmaceuticals I was being fed, she replied they were simply to keep me relaxed. This vagueness in her answer made me extremely uncomfortable. The pills were dished out at mealtimes in a tiny Dixie cup, and my inquisitive mind was intrigued by the clientele consuming these pharmaceuticals. For some time prior, I had been led to believe that getting high was both wrong and illegal, yet as I looked around, the people I was taught to respect, those being my elders and people from all trades and professions, were gobbling up the pills like candy. Some would trade and some would double up by purchasing someone else's medication. Was it just me or was it them who were messed up? The very moment of that realization I stopped ingesting the pharmaceuticals and started flushing them.

Another form of therapy that some patients were experiencing was Shock Therapy. That's right, an electrical current blasted through your skull in an attempt to rectify God knows what. Now my thoughts were not of my own well-being but of the barbaric methods used not only to indoctrinate but to suppress the human mind and will. There was one individual in particular who shared his experience of Shock Therapy with me. He was around 40 years old and was a professional by trade. Several times a week, he would be escorted to the "shock chamber" for a dose of good ol' Mother Nature. This guy anxiously awaited his treatments because of the buzz he received from it.

One morning as he was wheeled away, he turned to look me in the eye, then gave a smile similar to that of a child at Christmas time. Disgusted doesn't even come close to how I felt at that very moment. Within several minutes, I noticed the overhead lights flickering in my room and realized he had been cooked. Now I was anxiously awaiting his return. The interns wheeled him into the room and placed him in his bed. He couldn't move outside of turning his head to face me. A stupid grin stretched his lips from ear to ear and his eyes were the color of beets. Like a mindless helpless vegetable he lay there. This man had been cooked, fried to a crisp like bacon and was loving every minute of it. That was my cue to get the hell out of here.

Group talk sessions were extremely uncomfortable not only for myself but for all in attendance. We were seated in a large circle of around 20 people. When the doctor asked who would like to start, the air filled with a quiet tensity of silence. No one wanted to put their heart on their sleeve before a room full of strangers, especially not me. Eventually one brave soul would muster up the anal fortitude to melt before their fellow inmates. I was surprised to find that most of the patients that shared their story were victims of sexual abuse, men and women alike. A tragic misfortune in their life turned into a ghastly nightmare that haunted away every living second of their existence. Abuse begets abuse so many of these people then reciprocated their experience on the ones they loved. The more I learned of their troubles, the more I understood my own. My heart filled with compassion for these souls because I knew they were just like me- troubled.

My turn had come to bear my soul, not by pressure but by conscious choice. I pried away the lump from the back of my throat, took a deep breath and began. My story was entirely about Philip's death and my reaction to it. My listeners experienced the entire tragedy as though they were actually there. I shared it all, absolute truth about what happened that day. Now it was not only God and myself who were witness to the accident, but a roomful of people I didn't know and probably would never see again. The room erupted with sobbing faces as each of my newfound confidents shared their compassion with me. My secret was revealed like a Catholic confession. My heart weighed lighter in this first step towards personal atonement. I had experienced a release. The next step was to enlighten my parents to the truth.

A couple of days after my confession, I requested to be released of my own free will. In my mind, I was healed although the doctor was of another opinion. In fact, his last words as I left his office were, "You'll be back, Kevin." What a thing to say whether he was playing with my mind or speaking what he perceived to be the truth was irrelevant. There was no way on earth I would ever allow myself to be put in that position again- never. I was going home to make my peace then life would be grand. All I had to do was be brutally honest with my family then all would be well. Simple, right?

My homecoming wasn't much of an affair, just mom, dad and myself. I guess through embarrassment, they didn't let the cat out of the bag as to what had happened. On the other hand, I believe this to be the right choice because I wasn't interested in hearing all the rumors of how I'd gone psycho and end up in some looney bin. People can be extremely cruel through their choice of words.

Many tears were shed that evening as we three consoled each other. My parents offered all the moral support I would need to get my life on track. Once again college came up and the commitment to provide whatever education I desired. There was a real feeling of warmth between us, something I had not experienced for quite some time; however, something was still not right. A fear still existed within me - a fear that paralyzed me from telling the truth about the accident. Why was it that I could confess to a room full of strangers and not to the people near to me? No matter how hard I tried, I could not muster up the courage. Maybe it was a fear of confrontation. Maybe it was the fear of "being a bad boy" or for "speaking out to my elders." Whatever it was that stifled my voice, my truth, I could not open up no matter what. At the end of the evening, hugs were shared and we retired to bed.

During the next week, life seemed completely different. The way I interpreted my friends for example. Now I'm not saying these were bad people, but the fact is many of them were using me for my drugs and I was using all of the women for sex and trades. It dawned on me that none of the people I called friends were true friends at all. My girlfriend, for example, was now sleeping with one of my friends. When she discovered where I had been, her interest turned elsewhere. What kind of love was that? The more I looked around my environment, the one I had created, the more I disliked it. Change was inevitable.

The new school year was a ways off so I decided to check out the local manpower office in the meantime. There were loads of jobs to be had, all with the base wage of $5 per hour. The evidence now became fact that higher income is directly associated with higher education and personal value-added. Searching through the various ads, I noticed a flyer for Welder- Fitter training sponsored by the manpower office. This would be my new beginning. I had heard that licensed welders made excellent money, especially if they worked on the Alberta Pipeline. Taking the notice from the board I set up an appointment with one of the job counselors for later that afternoon.

The excitement of life and living was back in my veins! The course was 40 weeks in length and came with supplemental pay as well. Since I had no unemployment insurance coming in, I was given the minimum allowance of $50 every two weeks. It wasn't much but it was free money. That evening, I sat my folks down and explained with great excitement what I was about to do. Understand, at one point in my life I was an academic achiever, in other words, damn smart. Although I was excited I could see disappointment in the eyes of my parents, especially my father, the look of "you're better than that, Kevin". The words were never actually stated but the feeling was there. A mild congratulation was in order so dad took us out for dinner.

CHAPTER 7

Deep within myself, I knew I longed for bigger and better prospects for my life, but this was a starting point. The local college was full of life, and I soon blended right in. Our class was small—15 or so people—so it was easy to make new friends. Now, more than ever, I drove myself hard to excel. Was I looking to achieve an education, to prove something to myself, or even bigger, to Mom and Dad? I didn't know, and it didn't matter. I found theory to be child's play and, therefore, aced all the written tests and exams. Practical was another story. The withdrawal from alcohol and drugs left me quite shaky, so attempting to maintain a constant arc became quite challenging.

Of the entire class, there were four students who really had it down. Their welds were clean and flawless, which is what I desired. What better way to learn something than from someone who has the ability to do it, I thought. Sounds fair, right? I approached each of the four students to learn their secret. Only one of them, Larry, came by it honestly. The other three used outside influences to instill creativity and calmness of hand. You guessed it—drugs. I began to wonder if every success was achieved by giving something up, be it time with family or mental and physical health. Any way I looked at it, this life still sucked.

For the next few weeks, I refused to induce this calmness at the cost of my personal well-being. At the same time, my welding became worse. I was definitely putting the square peg in a round hole. I was extremely grouchy and irritable because I saw myself as a failure, even at something as simple as welding. There was no thinking involved in welding—you just do it, like coloring between the lines. This was pathetic, I thought. I was pathetic, came the ego again. There was no way I would allow myself the indignity of failing at something so simple, so I approached Gord, a student my own age, and asked if he had something to smoke. Gord pulled out a small vial from his pocket and gave me a smile only a stoner would appreciate.

"A little hash oil oughta do the trick," he proclaimed. We both dropped our welding shields into place, and Gord struck an arc. Once the metal pallet was glowing like an ember, we raised our shields, and he cautiously placed a small globule of the oil upon it. A puff of smoke shot up from the pallet, and I hesitantly inhaled the euphoric drug with ease. An instant rush came upon me like a wave of destruction, rendering me helpless to my surroundings. A flurry of questions and thoughts bombarded my mind like an invasion from within. Gord grabbed me by the shoulder and questioned my ability to move.

"Kevin, are you alright? Kevin!"

With a shake of my head, I came to my senses. A quick, unfocused nod to Gord reassured him that everything was cool. My booth was right next to his, so I didn't have far to meander. I felt paranoid yet calm. I jerked my shield into place, then struck an arc. To my surprise, I was absolutely graceful. The slag fell away like a peel from a banana, revealing a perfect beaded weld. I showered in the glory of this success, yet part of me felt ashamed for what I had done to achieve this success. Right there and then, I vowed that drugs would once again be a part of my life, but under strict supervision—by myself, and only under certain circumstances, that is, when I was welding. I had achieved victory through defeat that day.

The company my father worked for was a supplier of safety equipment for numerous industries, including the welding industry. It wasn't long before I was the guy with all the cool stuff. From masks and shields to gold-plated lenses, gloves to aprons, quivers to goggles—I had it all. I was the techno geek of my class, and I loved it! I loved the attention. I even began to dress differently to reflect my uniqueness. Everything I wore was black—black leather jacket, black jeans, black shirt, black buckled engineer boots, black leather hat, and even black underwear. I was nicknamed "Black Jack Shellac" by my fellow students and had absolutely no qualms about it.

I now had several female students from different programs taking notice, most likely because I came across as "the bad boy." I was in my element. I had become more than just the top student—I had become a badass babe magnet because of my uniqueness. My popularity with the opposite sex had become so prevalent that my mother refused to take any more phone calls for me because she couldn't keep track of whom I was with and not with. In actuality, this thoroughly disgusted her because she knew I was sleeping with all of them. It didn't bother me because I was getting the female attention I craved, while getting even with the female race whom I thought had abandoned me, taking my heart with them. I had become stone-cold towards women—no feelings, no emotion, and no respect.

My drug addiction kicked into full swing for several reasons. The calming effect allowed me to create welds as smooth as a pearl, the guys in my class respected me—or so I thought—because I was a party animal, and the college girls were easy pickings because I was so cool to be with. How could they know a child deep within me was clamoring to get out?

College life exposed me to new drugs like LSD and Magic Mushrooms, which severely put me over the edge. My body and mind had turned into a testing ground for pharmaceuticals and hallucinogens. These harsher drugs transformed me into a beast. Mixed with a bottle of Wiser's Deluxe Whiskey, I became physically invincible and violent. One evening, at a friend's house party, a fellow student looked at my date the wrong way—I proceeded to invite him outside, where I beat him about the face and head until he was within moments of death. His face looked as though it had been hit by a car! The anger within me, which had accumulated over the past decade, was being released. Instead of the victim, I had become the inflictor. No more beatings to Kevin.

Twenty-six weeks into the course, the college faculty decided to graduate our class 14 weeks early. One of our classmates had it in for an instructor, so as a practical joke, he placed a "cherry bomb" firecracker inside a pipe that was used for instructional welding. The instructor struck an arc, ignited the cherry bomb, and ended up in the hospital. Class dismissed.

So here I am, back on the street again with no job, no money, and no self-respect. Every morning, I stood in line at the employment office in search of work. Several days' work here, a few weeks there, it all added up to a mountain of horse shit. I finally asked my mother to allow me the use of the car to look in neighboring towns. Shortly thereafter, I landed a position at what welders refer to as a "sweatshop." For reasons I will not get into, I'll refer to the shop as "John's Welding and Steel."

You know how you feel nervous the first day in a new job? Well, I was so nervous I burned up an entire metal stair project I was assigned to! The staircase was tacked and fitted; all I had to do was weld. Being unfamiliar with the equipment I was using, I cranked the AC gauge to a point that, when I struck my arc, the intensity of the current blew holes right through the metal flanging. What a way to start my first day. Bruce, my knowledgeable supervisor, corrected the fittings, adjusted the machine for me, and then assured me all was well.

Being new to the company, I had no intention of bringing my drug habits into the workplace. I'm not saying I quit; I just stayed clean at work. Surprisingly, my welds were perfected with a sober hand. There was, however, a coworker who knew all about the world of drugs, which means, needless to say, we became friends. As odd as it sounds, his name was Kevin as well. Kevin had access to drugs I had never heard of, much less used. He also knew some very nasty people. As for myself, I stuck with the usual drugs. Kevin had been with the company for several years, so the owner allowed him certain bonuses and incentives. One of his tasks, in return, was to train Tammy, the owner's daughter, in the use of some basic metal bending and punching machines. Tammy worked part-time in the shop, where her father could keep an eye on her. Apparently, Tammy was somewhat of a naughty girl. The owner had also hired Diane, her cousin, to chaperone Tammy in his absence.

Since Kevin and I had become fellow partiers, he took it upon himself to invite me over to Tammy's house one evening. Her father had left town for the evening, so inviting Kevin over sounded like a good plan. My part in this was to chaperone Kevin—why, I didn't know. Was he afraid of what he may do with the boss's daughter? We arrived sometime mid-evening, and to my surprise, they lived in one of our family's temporary homes in Whitby when I was a child. Tammy had food and alcohol laid out for us, and Kevin had the drugs, so I was set with the necessities I required.

With each drink and pipe load, I slipped deeper into oblivion. Against the main wall of the basement rec room was an enormous wall unit stocked with guns—lots of guns. There must have been 20, if not 25, weapons on the racks. Tammy knew where the key was hidden and thought it best to show off these pieces. A good portion of them were antiques, but tucked in below were numerous handguns and what appeared to be a fully automatic weapon. I wasn't familiar with all of the names, brands, and types, but one of the weapons I saw was one that literally sprayed bullets when the trigger was pulled. "Why the fuck did he have this?" I questioned. This was enough to give me the creeps. I pulled Kevin aside and shared my discomfort with him, but his reply was to catch the bus home if I didn't want to stay. Walking 15 miles drunk and stoned was not my idea of fun, so I shut my mouth, sat down on the couch, and passed out. Several hours later, Kevin woke me up, and we drove home.

I wasn't sure what happened between the two of them, but I know that I woke up naked, clothes scattered about the downstairs bedroom, and Diane lying nude beside me in the bed. I had been sexually violated while passed out.

Two days later at work, the owner pulled Kevin and me into his office for a meeting. We both assumed it was about an upcoming project, as we had progressed to the point where we were the top welders of the company.

"Close the door behind you, sit down, and shut up," were the words growled out of this giant of a man. He reached into the top-right desk drawer, pulled out a .38-caliber revolver, slammed it on the desk with the barrel pointed toward us, and bellowed, "You screwed my teenage daughter! You have 15 minutes to clear out your tools, and if you're here any longer, I'll shoot you both in the face! Get the fuck out!!"

Fear? How about terror! Teenager? How could he?! Why did he? Kevin, you dumb son-of-a-bitch!

Within a heartbeat, I was out the office door, racing for my life and my locker. What I couldn't carry stayed behind because catching a bullet with my skull was not how I longed to end my life, especially for a crime I didn't commit. I had no vehicle, as I was commuting with another employee, so the shoe-leather express was my getaway mode of transportation. I never turned back that day for anything I left behind—not my tools, not my outstanding pay, and especially not Kevin.

Several months later, I heard that Kevin was arrested for robbing a local bank with some of his friends. The story goes that Kevin informed the police of his accomplices, which lessened his sentence. My guess is it also lessened his lifespan, as a contract was put out on his life. As for the sweatshop, apparently it was "repossessed" by creditors, if you know what I mean. Moving right along…

It was only a matter of weeks before I found other employment at a larger, more reputable fabrication shop. Solina Steel was still a distance from my home, but at least it was 5 miles closer. Still without a vehicle, I quickly found a ride to and from work. Joey lived several blocks from my home, which made commuting convenient for both of us. Joey was a couple of years younger than I and very pleasant to be around. The best thing about Joey was he didn't smoke, and he wasn't a drug addict. Finally, I had found someone I could be around without the need to get high. Joey, however, loved his beer. He wasn't an alcoholic by any means, but a cold beer after a hot day behind a shield was quite refreshing.

Structural steel and rigging were the specialties of Solina Steel. My job was simple—crank up the heat and burn stick all day. The beams and structures came to me tacked together, so all I had to do was weld on the dotted line. The pay was decent, and the work extremely simple. In fact, the work was so simple, I found myself dozing off on the job. My current qualifications allowed me to weld only, no actual fitting and fabricating, so I requested to be tested for vertical and overhead welding certification, as well as blueprint fitting. I don't mean to boast, but this field of work was not exactly rocket science for me. All three tests came and went with honors. My pay increased, as well as my taxes, so financially I was approximately $10 ahead per pay period, which was no great thrill to me. At least I had a more challenging position, which would keep me awake at work, right? Wrong.

Within two months, I was bored senseless. How was I to build my dreams when I hated my job and the pay wasn't much more than a general laborer behind a shovel? One morning, I brought some uppers to work just to stay awake for the day. I became so sick and tired of this job that I looked for ways to get out of work with pay. One day, I went as far as lifting my welding shield to expose my eyes to the rays of the arc, causing temporary blindness. Falling to the floor without sight, I was promptly taken to the hospital for medical attention. I had succeeded in getting the next two days off with pay.

You may ask yourself how I could do this to my eyes, but you must understand that, as far as I was concerned, no one loved me, including myself and God. Plus, I was going to burn in Hell anyway when I died, so it didn't really matter. I had reached the point where the only reason I remained with this company and career was to create an income that supported—or at least attempted to support—my habits. The questions brewing in the back of my mind were, "Why was my life spared?" and "What am I to do in this life?" These questions were definitely in the recesses of my mind because the answers weren't important enough to warrant taking action. Instead, I continued to party, and party hard.

As a young man in his 20s, being without a vehicle became quite embarrassing. I could tell my parents weren't overly keen on lending me their car because they knew I was drinking and driving, as well as sexually occupying the back bench seat. Nor did taxiing me around go over all that well, so I began shopping for a reliable, inexpensive yet cool car. I found a 1981 Oldsmobile that fit the bill, then went to the local bank for a loan. Since I had no credit history and my record of steady employment was virtually nonexistent, I was declined financing. Instead, I was offered a loan based on the guarantee of a cosignatory. This was a tremendous blow to my ego, as the sole signature I could think of was that of my father. This certainly was not an easy pill to swallow. How was I to get on the good side of my father after all the grief I had created for him?

I surmised that if I stayed clean and paid more attention to family life, Dad may go for it. It took three days to work up the gall to approach my father, and two days for him to reply. Within two weeks, I had $2,500 in my pocket, which purchased the car, paid for the insurance, and left a few dollars to party with. Within the month, I was involved in an alcohol-related accident that not only crushed the front end of my car but threatened the life of my three passengers.

Is my life ever going to turn around? I hated everything about my life—from my job to my friends to my family and including myself. I was in self-destruct mode with nowhere to turn. I began to question the option of leaving town with the understanding that I could leave these troubles behind. For every option I found at the employment center came the lack of qualifications. There was one option, however, that kept returning—join the army. This option did absolutely nothing for me, but what were my alternatives? I could stay where I was and experience an early death or allow the armed forces to train my habits and sorrows out of me. Boot camp won in a coin toss.

Bright and early the next morning, I enlisted at a local militia post. I was to be deployed for training within the week, which in reality made my skin crawl. I didn't want to be a pawn or a soldier, and I certainly didn't care to be indoctrinated by an overzealous male with bad breath! Don't get me wrong, I'm very proud of the men and women who serve their country—my country—but it's just not for me. My upbringing taught me not to fight but to "turn the other cheek." I couldn't fight even if I wanted to because of this. Stand up and stand out? Impossible, for it would involve breaking family vows.

Now that I was in, I avidly began to look for ways out. I even wondered if it was possible to go AWOL before even starting. Mom and Dad had no clue what I was embarking on, yet I'm sure they sensed my increased level of stress. Then it happened…

"Spring/Summer Employment. Great pay!! Lots of travel!! Must be physically fit. Call Lawrence at…"

This was it! This was my ticket away from this living hell. I dialed up Lawrence, and to my surprise, he lived right around the corner. I actually set up an interview for the next day without even asking what the work entailed. Based on the advertisement of great pay and lots of travel, I didn't care as long as I would be leaving Oshawa.

Lawrence was a bit of a funny duck, someone I remembered from high school. Regardless of his personality, I listened intently. The company was called Marcus Reforestation, and the work was tree planting. We would start in South Central Ontario around Cornwall in the beginning of April, then move to remote Northern Ontario come May. The job seemed simple enough—carry a bag of seedlings 6 to 8 inches tall and plant them every six feet. The pay was based on piece work; therefore, the more I planted, the more money I would make. Simple. Based on the description and details given, I could easily make $100 or more each day. Excited doesn't even scratch the surface of how I felt! Finally, I was going somewhere. Leaving town for five months would certainly open a world of avenues for me. In my mind's eye, I saw the lying, cheating, stealing, drinking, smoking, partying, sexual abuse, and self-destruction slipping away. Goodbye Army, hello reforestation!

When I informed my parents of my decision, I'm not sure they were all that pleased because it wasn't what they had planned for my life. To me, it didn't matter one way or the other what they thought or felt, because I had made my decision to go—and go I did, before the Army caught up with me.

CHAPTER 8

The fundamentals of tree planting in Southeastern Ontario: take two steps forward, make two insertions with the special shovel forming a "V" cut, fold back the sod, take a seedling from the hip bags, placing it in the hole, roots straight down, then fold the sod back covering the stock of the tree to what's called the collar. With the heel of your boot, place enough pressure down on the sod, thus giving enough compaction to remove all air pockets and hold the seedling upright. Repeat, repeat, repeat...

In reality, here are the fundamentals according to experience: take two steps forward, jab with a dull shovel, and hit a rock— "clang!" Move slightly to the side for new placement and hit clay. Take a small step forward or backward and the spacing is off, which throws off the density of trees per acre. Now that we've found proper placement, remove the seedling to discover the length of the roots exceeds the depth of the hole. Option A: dig a deeper hole. Result: minimal production equating to minimal pay. Option B: discreetly cut the roots to accommodate the depth of the hole. Result: maximum production but finable penalty offense if caught. Repeat, repeat, repeat...

Now that you've finished your very first load of seedlings, leave your shovel at your last planted tree and return to the cache for another load. Gently place the waterlogged seedlings into your bags, turn to face your track of land, and locate your shovel in a sea of waist-high grass. Yes, the shovel is brown, and no, there is no flagged trail or visible shovel.

Now let's discuss the "Meal Program." Under the terms of employment, three meals per day are provided at a cost of $13 per day and to be deducted directly from your paycheck. The contractor was to supply all necessary cookware and foodstuffs. Meals were to be of sufficient nutritional value to sustain the energy level required for such physically demanding work. Sounds like good old mom's home cooking, right? Well, here it is—the tree planter special: breakfast, 5:00 AM—cold cereal and yogurt. Lunch—as taken—bleached white bread, peanut butter, choice of jams or honey, two pieces of fruit. Dinner—whenever—I think Kraft dinner, raw carrots, one portion of meatloaf or one pork chop. After-dinner snack—whatever you buy with your own damn money.

Oh, and by the way, you do all your own cooking and cleaning. Is this beginning to sound like a chain gang? Allow me to do some basic math for you.

At $0.07 per planted tree based on 100% pay after quality inspection, it takes 185 trees to pay for food. Did I mention that we were staying in cabins at an additional cost of $20 per day? Allow me to add this to our total. $20 per day equates to 285 planted seedlings. Basic math: 185 trees to eat, 285 trees to get away from the rain, the cold, and the bugs equals 470 trees per day just to live. It gets better yet because for the first week, your average is 600 to 800 trees per day. The big bucks are starting to flow now! Week one: you plant 5,600 trees maximum, minus 3,290 trees for food and lodging, leaving 2,310 trees at $0.07 cents each, giving a grand weekly income, pre-tax, of $161.70. It was time for a powwow with Lawrence, our supervisor.

The selling feature of this job was the ability to generate $100 or more every day. At $0.07 per tree, that's almost 1,500 trees per day—almost double what we were planting in a 12 to 14-hour workday. I made more money hoeing cabbages for $5 per hour! Lawrence's only comeback was, "Work harder, I did it." This situation had become totally sickening. A solution to this dilemma would soon reveal itself.

A fellow planter, Don, who was a good friend of mine and also escaping his own perils, joined me for a late-night stroll to discuss our options. Quitting to return to our man-made hell was out of the question, so there had to be a way to mass-produce. Don was quite mathematically inclined, so he calculated the maximum density of trees allowable per acre, then added in a fudge factor for defective trees. These calculations gave us a sizable leeway to our advantage, bringing us closer to the target. My part was to figure out how to physically speed up production.

The first action was perfecting the shovel. I shortened the dowel by 18 inches, then used duct tape to form a grip handle. After that, I had both edges of the head sharpened by the owner of the cabins. This would make sod cutting somewhat quicker. The roots were definitely a challenge, so I personally sharpened two pocket knives for pruning. When we loaded up, we would take time to separate each bundle, then comb the roots with our fingers. After a quick peek over the shoulder, the roots were cut to the length of the shovel blade, and the remainder placed in the bottom of the tree bag with the rest of the sludge. Once in the field, the excess roots were disposed of. These two actions increased productivity to a degree, yet still left us short of our goal.

Since Don and I planted together, the only other surmisable tactic was to stash the remainder of the trees. Mathematically, we had the variance, so why not? By the end of week two, production had doubled. We didn't hit the target every day because some days we would drive for two hours just to get to the site, then all 20 planters would literally attack the land. Upon completion, we drove further out and did it all over again. For the most part, we were averaging $70 per day. This was a far cry from $162 for the week.

Lawrence was suddenly pleased with our progress because, apparently, his earnings were reflective of our earnings. As for the other planters, they all wanted to know our secret of success. Needless to say, it was our secret. There were four weeks of spring planting, and for those who excelled, came the "privilege" of staying on to plant in the North Country. The North Country was fabled for its sand flats and $200 to $300 days. If it was a competition to retain the job, Don and I were sure to watch out for number one.

One evening, Don and I sat down along the shores of the St. Lawrence River and discussed business and our options for advancement. Neither of us could understand how one was to earn $100 every day given the management and planning of the outfit. With numerous planters per section of land, it was mathematically impossible to achieve this unless all of the other planters remained at the side of the road. The French crew always had their own agenda—land, housing, and food benefits—and maximum per day.

As Don and I were the top producers of our crew, we proposed to Lawrence that he give us our own parcel of land at the beginning of the day and pick us up at the end of the day. In Lawrence's mind, this was not an option. He couldn't seem to wrap his mind around the concept of multiple streams of production, which in turn would move up the contract completion date. I think Lawrence had burned more brain cells from drug use than I had. The result of the conversation was he would allow us to work alongside the French crew, provided it was acceptable with them. This was better than a kick in the pants, I guess. Our only thought was how would our tactics of production fit in with the new work arrangement?

We had arrived at a point in the contract that required moving camp to the next township as commuting distances to planting blocks did not justify our current location. Our next home was a motel some 150 miles away. Planting was to commence in three days, which allowed ample time for relocation. As a "reward," we were each given a $100 advance on our pay. The unanimous decision was to go into town, Cornwall to be exact, for a few drinks, do our laundry, and devour some real food. Once everyone was accounted for, we crowded into the vans and headed out.

Cornwall is a very beautiful town boasting some extravagant Victorian homes. The town exuded history and landmarks, giving me a sense of peace about where I was and the journey I had chosen. I decided to spend some time alone in reflection, so I told the others I would meet up with them at the laundromat in a couple of hours. It had been some time since I had last stood outside the box and looked in—actually, since my visit to the hospital a few years earlier.

Once again, I had come to a point in my life of decisions— decisions of who I desired to become and what place I was to fill in this world. Given my past history, I was technically undereducated, yet experientially over-educated in this game of life. Questions came at me like a mid-December flurry.

"Who am I now? Where am I going? Is that my choice or one to please my parents? Are your choices based on fear or hope? Do you desire to go to school? If so, which school and for what?"

A never-ending stream of questions with a waterfall of "I'm not sure" answers and "What ifs." Amongst the entourage of questions, one frightening truth kept popping up—"Kevin, do you love yourself?" Two answers automatically followed every time. My mind would answer, "Of course I do," yet my heart would deny the answer. Each time I would force this disturbing thought away, yet each time it returned like a paddleball. The stronger the force of rejection, the quicker and harder it would return. My heart was throbbing, and I began to sweat profusely until I finally shouted, "Stop!" In a hazy panic, I started to run for shelter. I had truly become lost in life and was unsure which way to turn. One thing was for sure—I wanted out.

It wasn't long before I located the laundromat, only to find that I was too late. Directions were left at the front counter of where I could meet the gang, so I didn't bother sticking around to do my own laundry. The pub was five or six blocks away, and since I had been running my entire life, I was there in a heartbeat. For those of you who have been known to tip a glass or two, do you remember the darkest, dingiest, sleaziest bar in town? You know the one—no windows, dim lighting, and sauced with the smell of despair? Well, this was definitely Cornwall's finest bar.

Once inside, I realized what the decision-making process entailed—greasy food, cheap drinks, and strippers. Obviously, this is why only six planters were there and the rest had gone back to pack up camp. Matt, Steve, Don, Patrick, Sleepy, and of course, Lawrence, were right at ringside howling like a pack of wild dogs. Was my life destined to be like this? Had I chosen this life in order to experience pain and hardship? I pulled up a chair at the table behind the others and sat with my back against the post. Paranoia or a means of defense?

At first, the guys all ridiculed me for my behavior, but soon they started to drift over to my table, as did the girls. My disgust was appeased by the ale as I slipped into oblivion. Round after round, toast after toast, the badgering questions of self faded away. It was as though I was there but wasn't really there because I suddenly realized I was the only one there! How long had I sat there, and where the hell were the others? No sooner had this thought crossed my mind when Patrick tapped me on the shoulder from behind.

"Kevin, come with me. You gotta see this!" I poured myself out of the chair and staggered behind Patrick out the door.

It was close to midnight and raining like I'd never seen before. We made our way across the street, then through a field to a large factory of some sort. Patrick pried open the rusty metal door, and we slipped inside. All but Lawrence were awaiting me. Breaking and entering is a felony offense where I come from, and since I had already seen a jail from the inside on several occasions, I had no intention of returning. The guys begged and pleaded with me to wait for them, so I agreed but only for five minutes. I don't remember much of what went on inside, but I do remember what was going on outside. A silent alarm had triggered, and the federales had arrived with lights flashing.

I sounded my own alarm while scrambling through the factory looking for a back door. Don was hot on my heels as I crashed through a utility door and raced through the back lot and over the chain-link fence, tearing my pant leg on the top wire. We had made it a block from the scene when the police drove around the corner. Scared straight, we halted to a slow walk and made like we were out for a stroll. The police car stopped, doors flung open, then, "Hands behind your heads and down on the ground—now!"

I'm told that the Cornwall jail is one of the oldest, if not
the oldest, standing jails in Canada. It was easy to understand
why, because this place was a fortress. The walls were built from
mortared stone blocks rising two to three stories in height, and yes,
there was barbed wire cresting the top of the wall. We were locked
up together in a small, white-washed cell with a wooden table and
two benches in the middle, which took up the majority of the
room. There was one window constructed into the stone wall that
was the depth of the thickness of the stone, which was just enough
for a body to completely sit in the windowsill. The window came to
a point at the top like the windows you see in a church, except this
window was protected by a heavy-gauge iron mesh.

This perch had become Matt's preferred place of contemplation.
From sunrise to sunset, Matt would bury himself in thought
within the depths of the window, silent to all around him. Matt
had always been quiet on the outside but had become mute on
the inside. His freedom of expression was offered through his
enchanting mystical melodies by Jethro Tull flowing through
the breath of his flute. Here, there were no serenades or utopian
melodies, only loneliness and despair.

Within our confinement, there were six smaller chambers in
which we slept. Each room had a steel bar door and a cot that took
up the entire floor space. The ceiling was just high enough that
the average person could stand up, so the only thing I could do in
my cage was sleep, because there wasn't room to do anything else.
Our home was whitewashed and barren; we had no control over
anything, including when to lie down. This was by far the eeriest
place I'd ever been. I wondered about the other prisoners who had
shared this chamber and what we had in common. I worked at
convincing myself that I was a good person, only to be overruled by
an ego that declared war on this lifetime. My internal strength had

been depleted, so I surrendered—I was a bad person, and my life was worth nothing. I had been in this mindset before, which led me only to self-destruction; this was a day of recognition.

One by one, we were given courtyard privileges, myself being the last to go. The guard cuffed my hands behind my back and accompanied me through a series of hallways and gates leading to the courtyard below. The cuffs were removed, and once outside, I was offered a basketball and a cigarette. "You have one hour, Mr. Hanna, make good use of it," were the only words muttered by the guard.

So here I am, incarcerated in a historical dungeon, standing alone outside in the rain with a basketball in one hand and a cigarette in the other. There are no communicable words to string together that could describe how messed-up the emotional and mental state I had created felt like. Spiritual death seemed inevitable to me. Although I believed it to be a futile attempt at resurrection, I dropped to my knees and began to pray to a God I wasn't sure existed for forgiveness and release from my purgatory. Within three days, we were all released on a conditional discharge, the condition being "keep the peace and be of good behavior" for the next 12 months and never return to Cornwall. Maybe there was a God, and He was listening....

Our employer had been informed of our whereabouts during our time of incarceration and had agreed to keep us on, although we were to find our own way to the next base camp. Our combined funds were insufficient for all of us to ride the bus to the new location but were sufficient to get us from the next township on. After several hours of walking in total silence, the six of us connected with the bus and slept the duration of the trip. Upon arrival, we were pulled aside by our employer and given the riot act. As it turned out, our discharge was based on our employment and the fact that the contract completion date was quickly approaching. At this point in the game, recruiting and training six new planters would create a delay in production, resulting in contract penalties. It was in the best interests of both parties to move beyond this challenge and complete the terms agreed upon. Within 10 days, the contract was complete, and we were all homeward bound.

On the eve of our departure, Matt serenaded the moon and stars till the wee hours of the morning as melodies created by Jethro Tull whispered through the crisp night air. I never saw or heard from Matt again.

CHAPTER 9

Although I had been away for only several quick weeks, Oshawa seemed different to me—almost brighter somehow. I was sensing relief in my being and what may have been faith, but the desire to leave was inherent. I called the employer and shared with him my desire to stay on as a planter and move north for the summer. After reviewing my planting statistics, he agreed to keep me on under the same conditions granted by the judge—stay out of trouble. To my surprise, he kept all of us on and hired several new recruits, including my friend Alan.

The next contract was one week away, so we had plenty of time to stock up. We were off to the wild frontier, which required certain essentials like bug protection, proper boots, a tent, sleeping gear, rain gear, and so on. Instead of giving us the remainder of our pay from the previous contract, we were each given a small advance, barely enough to cover our supplies. Some of my personal supplies were given to me by my father, as he was in the safety business, so I had money left over to purchase a tin of tobacco and some goodies. Don owned a car, so Alan and I rode with him, paying for gas along the way.

Longlac was our destination this time, a forestry town with an extremely high First Nations to Caucasian ratio. I'd always dreamed as a boy of being an Indian. Actually, I could have been a cowboy or an Indian at that age, but I always preferred the good guys—the Indians.

Longlac wasn't quite what I had expected. A mere blink of an eye and you were through it. The largest part of the development was the reserve. The standards of living were absolutely atrocious—abandoned vehicles scattered about, burnt-out homes as numerous as the vehicles, and the homes that were standing were nothing more than clapboard shacks. It wasn't the housing so much that nauseated me as it was the activities of the children. Primary-grade children were sniffing glue from paper bags, hiding between the dwellings. Suddenly, my troubles seemed trivial compared to the bleak future of these children. I despised being white because these people were of the land and had been here long before any white man stepped off the boat, until they were basically evicted and abandoned, then left for dead—and not of their own choosing. Atrocious. The government gave itself and its agents the "right" to do so under "The Indian Act of 1876." And you think Hitler was bad?

This contract was only two weeks in length, so we stayed at the town motel and dined at the restaurant across the highway. The sleeping arrangements were comfortable, and the food was decent, but the planting conditions were horrendous. The tract of land looked as though a tornado had come through, devastating everything in its path. Slash and debris were everywhere. The poplars and aspens were all uprooted, creating obstacles that were sometimes several feet high. The only planters among us experienced in this type of ground were the French planters; the rest of us stood in awe. Don and I knew exactly how production levels would be reached—root preparation and stashing. How else could it be done? The pay plan was the same, but the terrain was worse. This was definitely a covert operation.

As harsh as the land seemed to be, I found it possible to make reverence with it. Each block of land was large enough to keep four planters busy for three days without even seeing each other. Alan, Don, Paula, and myself were teamed up for our assignment. Al never lasted three days before quitting. Did he know something I didn't, or was he merely lacking courage and fortitude? I think the latter, as Al had been somewhat of an "unsavory" individual for as long as I knew him. With just the three of us left in the crew, we each picked a focal point and staked our claim. My choice was along the back perimeter so that I could have the experience of solitude, not to mention stash a few bundles of trees.

There must have been something mysterious about this block of land because within the first couple of days, Don also resigned as a planter and took on the role of delivery person/maintenance man, and Paula was caught stashing trees. Had we disturbed the spirit of the land or maybe an ancient burial ground? I'm not sure, but suddenly I was alone. Good or bad, I had no definition for it—it just was. I requested to remain the sole planter in this block with no hesitation or restriction from Lawrence. This had become a task or challenge I had to complete. The challenge was personal, to find out or discover who I was. Twelve hours per day of solitude has a way of surfacing issues and character traits, both good and bad. Sometimes fear and loneliness would creep in, but for the most part, I was able to tear up some of the masks I had chosen to wear.

Feelings of resentment towards my parents arose quite frequently during my retreat. Since Philip's death, Mom had shown me no physical attention, nor had either parent taken any measure to be involved with me in sports or academics. The resolution had always been, "Kevin, you should speak with a counselor as you're not well." Well, no kidding! I wasn't hiding out in a Northern Boreal Forest for the good of my health; I desired love and affection. I wanted to belong, to know how much I mattered. The more I pondered, the more resentment would turn to anger. I loved my family due to genetics, yet I hated them at the same time. For all I knew, they were glad to have me gone. To this day, I have never expressed those thoughts and feelings to my family, and those thoughts of yesteryear never take root in my heart anymore.

Absolutely every challenge I faced or created was related to Philip's death. I knew this was the root, but I wasn't able to connect the pieces. The accident was over a decade ago, and I had moved beyond it—or had I? Anyway, this contract came and went like a bolt of lightning. We would be moving camp again, but first, we would travel back to Oshawa for another break. Personally, this trip back and forth seemed redundant, as our new camp would be one hour further up the highway to Geraldton. The next contract was only several days away, so why waste time and money on an unnecessary trip? Our employer was a decent fellow, yet somewhat confusing in his business actions.

A celebration of completion was in order, so with cash advances in hand, off to the liquor store we marched. This contract was significantly more challenging than those of Southern Ontario, so we were determined to get inebriated. Alcohol, beer in particular, was like Kool-Aid to me, so I purchased a flat and went to work. The entire evening is still a blur to me, though I do remember singing, dancing, and swimming around midnight. I also remember waking up with Jeanne. Jeanne was one of the French planters. She was a very earthy type of girl, to the point of being a hippie. She loved her Reggae music, accompanied with some of Quebec's finest weed. She wasn't physically beautiful—just honest and plain. How or why I ended up beside her was beyond me. I sneaked out of the bed and quietly headed for the door. Guilt, shame, and disgust were the ingredients in my hangover mixing bowl of feelings. I longed for a rock to crawl under and hibernate.

There's no feeling comparable to that of wondering what you did or said the night before. Was I the life of the party or a complete asshole? Alcohol is nothing more than a thief of reality and identity. It embellishes the ego and sacrifices the soul; a poison in and of itself. For some unknown reason, my room was the infirmary for the majority of the crew. Apparently, I wasn't the only one experiencing the day-after-the-night-before blues. Why is it that young people congratulate themselves on how drunk they were the night before? It's like a sense of pride to boast and brag about how much of an idiot you had become. I was beyond that stage because I knew I had a substance abuse problem, among other horrible traits. Inwardly, I was begging for a shoulder to cry on, yet outwardly I had become a cold, insensitive prick. I didn't give a rat's ass about anyone or anything, and why should I? As far as I knew, I was already destined to burn in Hell, and in actuality, this was my Hell.

Don was the only person to comment on my whereabouts the night before, which brought some relief to my aching soul. I couldn't change what happened, so why grieve over it? Within a couple of hours, all the gear was loaded, and we were ready to move. The moment of truth had come, for Jeanne stood beside the truck waiting to speak with me. I couldn't tell if it was a nervous sweat or an embarrassment sweat I was experiencing, but I do know it was challenging to look Jeanne in the eyes.

"It's OK, Kevin. We had a great time last night, so let's leave it at that. I'll see you in a few days."

I didn't so much as mutter a word as Jeanne climbed into the truck and drove off. Apparently, the festivities of the previous night were exactly that—and nothing more. There was no commitment or guilt attached to our actions, which was a relief to me because I couldn't remember the details anyway. The best part was, Jeanne didn't expect anything from me.

CHAPTER 10

OCTOBER 21, 2021 RETURN TO WRITING

Sitting in my office on a dreary, rainy fall day on Vancouver Island, while trying to recover from the damage caused by a tragic motorcycle accident, I have just transcribed my writings of many moons before to paper. I found my memoirs safely secured in a leather portfolio; the writings scribed onto at least a dozen different types of paper. Fortunately, my Libran mind numbered and categorized the notes before putting them to bed almost 20 years ago.

Reading and then rereading my scribblings and notes at this stage in my life didn't faze me emotionally as much as I would have thought it would, but I felt more compassion for the Kevin I was during those moments in my life. This is a massive shift in self-recognition, self-awareness, self-forgiveness, and self-love.

Amongst my notes, I found some very unique scribblings that were written one pitiful night when I was living in a basement in Whistler. Some of you may recall the book series called

"Conversations with God" (Neale Donald Walsh)—well, this writing was an exercise from one of the books. I had asked myself a question, a very tough question, and then gave the pen to my left hand and awaited an answer (I am right-handed). Tears flowed like a waterfall, and the words were not my own. Thinking of it now, I can see and feel and believe where the words and the answer came from, with a smile on my face stretched ear to ear. OK, enough about that—maybe another book? On with the journey...

The summer plant started off with a bang before the first root had been clipped. I decided to rent a small hatchback for this next contract so I could pack what I wanted and be able to leave should the occasion arise. The trip north consisted of Don, Pat, and myself. Day one, we drove as far as Hurst, Ontario (last stop on the road to nowhere) and decided to spend the night at a roadside motel. Pat didn't have the funds to pitch in, so Don and I split the room, and Pat slept in the back of the car. The next morning after breakfast, we packed up and headed out. We weren't but fifteen miles down the road when what looked like the entire O.P.P. Hurst Detachment (Ontario Provincial Police) had us pulled to the side of the highway and handcuffed! Seriously? It just so happened that when Pat slept in the car the night before, he borrowed a blanket from the room, but didn't give it back before we left. All this for a blanket—I thought I'd seen everything.

The contract was successful, though colorful along the way— like getting into a bar fight in Geraldton because I had a Mohawk hairstyle and we were in a First Nations-dominated bar or being heli-evacuated for medical attention due to a fall while planting "Plot Armageddon." I had become a homing signal for misfits, drama, criminal activity, and flat-out B.S.

By the end of the contract, Jeanne and I had developed mutual admiration, and upon being given the invitation to move east at the end of the summer, I agreed without hesitation. I had nothing of note or value left in Oshawa—or Ontario, for that matter. Besides, I was exhausted from looking over my shoulder for the next attack of retaliation created by the inexcusable actions I had taken throughout my teens.

Leaving Oshawa was more of an escape than a departure. Jeanne and her sister Lorri arrived mid-morning after Mom had left for town, and I anxiously threw my "Surplus Army Duffle Bag," chock-full of what little I had, into the open hatch of their vehicle. Buckled in and loaded, off we went.

The night before, I had written a letter to Mom attempting to explain my current actions and the motives behind the move, and that leaving was best for everyone. I assured my mother—the one true inherent bond that still remained—that I would call her once I was settled in. We were destined for Grand-Mère, a tiny village a couple of hours east of Montreal, where Jeanne's family home was. From there, we would immediately create a plan for where to live and then work towards a place in the country until planting season began in the spring.

As my knowledge of the French language had miraculously vanished from my mind—even after seven years of classes, go figure—we opted for the multicultural metropolis of Montreal. One of Jeanne's planting friends spends snowy winters in the city installing pop-up shelters for vehicles, and as I had already met and planted with him, he gladly accepted me as a laborer. Within a couple of weeks, we were knocking out half a dozen or more installations every day, and at $40-$50 per installation, we were making some good cash! Feeling like my life had settled down, I called home.

My mother answered the phone after several rings, and I greeted her with a heartfelt "Hi Mom," to which she only responded, "Kevin?"

"Yes, it's me, Mom. I'm doing very well, settled in and working… and…" I was interrupted mid-update by tears. My mother blurted out, "Your father doesn't want you to come home or call anymore, Kevin."

A second, a minute, a heartbeat—how long was the dead air space? Long enough to hear "Goodbye" and "I love you."

If you have never encountered gut-wrenching shame to the point of mental and physical disability, then may I advise that you never enter this pit. A myriad of questions, statements, impulses, criticisms, self-deprecating thoughts, an on and on barrage every cell of your being until the only thing you can do is collapse, vomit, and pray that you were dead. In my mind, the entire 'conversation' boiled down to "We don't love you. We don't want you. Stay away forever."

In order for someone or something to have value to another, there must be, in some way, shape, or form, a level of love— even at a base level—in order to create a bond or connection. When someone or something is cast aside, that level of love has diminished, therefore canceling the bond or connection. Having been requested to refrain from any and all contact is nothing short of complete disassociation. I had been officially excommunicated from my family.

Emotionally numb, void, distant, or just plain crushed are the most adequate descriptive words for how I felt, lying in a pool of my own vomit without even being drunk. None of this would be happening if I hadn't killed Philip...

CHAPTER 11

Montreal was a short-lived stay, lasting less than a year. Montreal fascinated me far more than Toronto. In Montreal, buskers played tunes in the Metro Station (subway), and the entire subway was clean and free of debris and graffiti. The Toronto subway system was a nightmare and very dangerous—trash everywhere, with loads of junkies and beggars. Even I avoided the subway in Toronto for fear of getting robbed, though I owned nothing, or even murdered, though it would have been welcomed at the time.

The city center of Montreal also offered multicultural experiences, probably with more languages than just French—ones I hadn't even heard before. As much fun and experiential as Montreal was, it was still a metropolis, while Jeanne and I both longed for a quieter life in the country, closer to her family. Another major factor in our decision to move was housing—Montreal was at least twice as expensive for accommodation that would be a third the size of a residence elsewhere. After a few weeks of research, we found a spacious two-bedroom house with a full basement and a large lot backing onto wooded lands for $500/month. This was a no-brainer, and it was only a five-minute drive into Grand-Mère to visit with family. The tiny village of Hérouxville, Quebec, became my new home.

As it was springtime, Jeanne and I accepted employment with a reforestation company called "La Médéole," the second-largest planting outfit in the province. The owner, Guy Fortin, was the doppelganger of Chevy Chase—seriously. I couldn't look at Guy without a flash from *Second City* coming to mind!

It was an eye-opening experience working with Guy, as everything required for a successful season was provided and at a much better cost than that of Markus Reforestation. All the food we could eat at $13/day, equipment provided for free with the option to purchase, and plots of land situated in the same vicinity, meaning we moved camp maybe twice during the season. Everything was spot on.

The season passed by in a flash without any hitches or glitches. Then Jeanne had us set for Apple Picking Season in Frelighsburg, just south of Montreal along the border to Maine. Apple Season was a four-week contract, paid by the bin. It wasn't as well-paying as tree planting, but it provided the employment stamps required to collect Unemployment Insurance from fall through to the following spring, when planting opened again.

Picking was an experience in and of itself. The ladders were at least twenty feet long, tapering toward the top, with only a one-post leg in the front—an accident waiting to happen. I fell a lot, though without breaking anything like my neck! Personally, I tolerated it because it was necessary to sustain us through the winter months. Come fall, we both had our insurance established and were nestled into our cozy country cottage.

Jeanne came from a very staunch Catholic family, as most Quebecois do. She had six brothers and sisters, which was also very common there and then. Her dad was a logger who left for the winters, and when he arrived back home, there was another child. Birth control was a no-no, so it wasn't unusual for me to have friends who came from families of a dozen or more. One dear friend, "La Toc," came from a family of 21 kids. Their names? Jean, Jean Paul, Jean Claude, Jean Marc, Jean Pierre, Marie, Marie Claude, Marie Louise, and so on. I guess it made it easier—when called, at least three children would come!

Jeanne's youngest sister was Sophie. During the previous apple season, Sophie met an intriguing young man from Venezuela named David. David was slender, with a sparse goatee and a Spanish accent. His father was of European descent, and his mother was Venezuelan. David had been traveling abroad, or so he called it. It took no more than ten weeks from the day they met until wedding bells. Love or a Green Card? Exactly!

David and I were both outsiders in many ways—outsiders to the new family, to the French language and culture, but more importantly, we were both refugees, escaping from our respective traumas, tortures, and guilt. These similarities made us compatible comrades, but David's knowledge and expertise in his "field" were what truly cemented our friendship.

David's father's business in Venezuela was that of an Amazon bush pilot, catering to scientists, geologists, and the like, transporting them into remote airstrips within the Venezuelan Amazon. The operation was completely above board—except for David. Understand, this was the '80s, so bringing in a pound or so of "mota" (grass) or Coca leaves was unnoticeably easy for him. Now, with a Canadian passport, David saw it as a "get out of jail free" card.

Living in rural Quebec was right up my alley. No one spoke more than broken English, and I had only remnants of my school days' French, so communication required a translator. Yet, Quebecois hospitality stood out above all else—no matter whose home you visited, there was always warm food on the stove, beer (especially Laurantide, the big ones), and red wine. I could walk to the local dépanneur, buy one cigarette, a large Laurantide, and a bag of fresh cheese curds. Starvation or lack of camaraderie were never problems during my stay in Quebec.

David and I shared some interesting adventures. One of my favorites was during the beginning of our friendship. We were out on a regular hike, on a lovely fall day, in the "back forty," with some grub for the fire, wineskins, smokes, and, of course, a small brick of hashish. Hash was readily available in Quebec and very inexpensive.

After devouring our lunch and smoking a joint, David started talking about the treetops swaying in the breeze. For some reason, he figured he could climb one, get it swaying, and then jump to a neighboring tree. David insisted he'd done it before. So, up he shimmied. The top of the tree had maybe a four-inch diameter, but David started to gently sway. He was at least 40 feet above the ground, swaying on a toothpick, before he launched himself like a flying monkey.

It was like slow motion watching David hit the neighboring tree, fail to grab hold, and plummet down, hitting every branch on the way, before landing with a final "THUD!" It's still the stupidest and funniest thing I've ever seen.

David was alive, but he wasn't impressed with me. Why? Because I couldn't stop laughing! It was one of those uncontrollably funny moments. David left right after that, and I showed up at Sophie's an hour later, where David was already flat out on the floor.

Another favorite pastime of ours was going to "Spot 55," about 20 minutes down the highway, but only on Sunday nights. It was cheap night and Ladies' Night, so beer was 50 cents, and the women-to-men ratio was at least 4:1. David was a real Casanova, while I was just there for cheap drinks and dancing. Once the music started, I was on the floor, dancing with no inhibitions. By the end of the first song, I'd be surrounded by women. Yet, despite all the attention, I never committed any sexual acts with these women—it would have ruined the experience for me. I craved attention, not anything I had to hide or lie about.

It wasn't until one morning, well into my second year in Quebec, that I realized I'd fully absorbed the French language and mannerisms. I woke up realizing my dreams the night before had been entirely in French. I had picked up the slang, the vocabulary, and the body language. Those closest to me found it comical but respected the effort I put in. Given the province's threat to separate over French-English tensions, this effort worked in my favor. Now that I was truly bilingual, I was open to better opportunities, invitations, and friendships—like my friendship with Richard.

Richard was a couple of years my junior and had taken quite a shine to me. Richard didn't speak a word of English, so I became his tutor, and soon, his best friend. We also made an epic tree-planting duo while away in camp for the season. We gauged our speed and efficiency by the time it took to finish a bottle of Rémy Martin Cognac from the moment we arrived on site to the last tree planted. Cognac in our coffee thermos kept us going through the day, and when the bottle was gone, so was our workday. It wasn't the most traditional work method, but it worked for us.

What I didn't know about Richard at first was his winter occupation. Through his connections, he imported mushroom spores from Mexico and propagated them during the winter months in Old Quebec City. I'm talking about magic mushrooms, hallucinogens. If you want a mental image, just think of that peyote scene from the movie *"Young Guns"*. I had experimented with shrooms in the past, but nothing like what Richard had going.

It was the first week of May 1985, during the *Parc La Vérendrye, Racines Nues* contract. In a nutshell, this was the "Park-at-the-End-of-the-World" bare-root spring plant. We were truly at the end of civilization, where the gravel highway narrowed into a compacted, graded dirt road. This far north was about "P and P"—pulp and paper. You had black spruce in the swamps and muskegs, where if you stopped moving, the floating carpet would suck you beneath, never to be seen again. Occasionally, we'd find rare sand flats where we could plant pine plugs amongst endless fields of wild blueberries. But all the while, you had to scan the horizon for one of the smartest, blackest creatures you never want to meet: *Canis lupus*, the Canadian Timber Wolf.

Our camp was a good hour's drive up that runway-sized gravel highway into what felt like the land of never-ending twilight. The terrain was flat and dense, with no real landmarks, hills, or elevations. Just miles of endless, eye-level wilderness. The camp had all the usual requirements—flat land, clean water, and fire safety compliance. But this far into the wild, it also brought with it something different, something more mystical: the Raven.

This was my first experience this far north during planting season, and, as we soon found out, we couldn't plant right away— the ground was still too cold and frozen. The camp wasn't fully set up yet, and most of the crew hadn't arrived. But there were two "Organic Aficionados"—Ganja Farmers—who had shown up early, setting up camp by the rapids for access to fresh running water and fish. We quickly fell into routine, gathering firewood and prepping for the long days ahead.

There was one major problem—there wasn't any food.

None of us had planned for this delay, and I hadn't brought any food staples. Sure, I could trap, clean, and cook small game, but that wasn't the plan. We were expecting the camp to be fully stocked. But here we were—four broke, unshaven, hungry, and smelly tree planters, a couple of hours from the nearest town.

We scraped together enough money to last us a few days and set off for town to buy supplies. Groceries, gas, laundry, and, of course, the pub—all in one spot, as small towns tend to have everything you need in a single place.

We minimized our food list so we could maximize our beer budget. Noodles, potatoes, coffee, creamer, a case of water, and two flats of beer (because beer was cheaper than food this far north). We figured we were set for a few days.

Richard suggested we stop at the pub for a round of billiards before heading back. Why not? It was cheap night, after all. But that's when things went very wrong, very fast.

There were only six people in the pub, including us. The bartender, us four planters, and a young, attractive blonde sitting by herself. I felt a little dirty as we each tried to get her attention, but she gravitated toward me, the "square head" in a room full of "frogs" (as the French were called back then). I became her instructor of choice in billiards, which felt more protective than anything else.

It wasn't long before I realized we had been there longer than our budget allowed, and yet the pitchers of beer kept coming. Something didn't add up. I excused myself and pulled Richard aside to confront him about our rapidly growing tab.

With a chuckle, Richard led me outside to the trunk of his '70 Impala. Inside was a large, double-knotted black garbage bag.

"Open it up, Kev, and take a look," he whispered.

I had seen varying amounts of drugs before, but I wasn't prepared for this. Inside that bag was enough magic mushrooms to get an entire village high for a month!

Richard had made a deal with the bartender. We were trading mushrooms for everything—beer, snacks, whatever we needed. I could hardly believe it.

It didn't take long for our pub mates to catch wind of what was happening. And, as one would expect in such a scenario, things spiraled from there. Between the mushrooms, weed, and beer, we all descended into a haze of munchies and hallucinations. It was time to leave.

We stumbled into the Impala and sped off into the night. The Northern Lights, or Aurora Borealis, danced across the sky above us in a magnificent display, and in our mushroom-induced haze, it felt like the end of the world.

Half in and half out of consciousness, all of a sudden there was a deafening "BANG!"

The front passenger side of the car hit something hard, and suddenly, we were airborne. The Impala rolled, barrel-rolling left, end over end, until we landed roof-side down in the ditch.

I woke up hanging upside down by my seatbelt, dazed and confused. Not a word was spoken as we crawled out through shattered windows. Our belongings were scattered everywhere as everything except us was ejected from the car. I didn't want to know what had happened. I just wanted to sleep, so I lay down right there on the side of the road.

It wasn't long before we were rescued by a logging contractor who recognized us from the laundromat. Without asking any questions, he gave us a ride back to camp. We never spoke of that night again, nor did we hang out much for the rest of the contract. I kept working with Richard because we made a good team, but that was it.

That was also the last time I ever touched magic mushrooms.

A few weeks later, while doing laundry in town, I overheard a conversation about two teenagers who had been rushed to the hospital after overdosing on mushrooms. One of them, the bartender Richard had made the deal with, was still in ICU.

The guilt hit me like a ton of bricks. I couldn't plant properly for days. "What if this kid dies?" I thought. I couldn't shake it.

We finished the contract three days later, packed up, and left town. I've never looked back on that event until now, and to this day, I have no idea if the young man lived or died.

CHAPTER 12

It's interesting how simple it becomes to cache things away after prolonged exposure to traumas—things like secrets, lies, truths, and even abominations. It's like the 'inner sounding board' just stops feeling before registering what's going on. It's like having a filing box in your core that's labeled "TOXIC – DO NOT OPEN," and it's your vault of vulnerabilities that would cripple, if not kill you, if revealed. There is no heavier weight a person can shoulder than that of guilt and shame.

On the flip side of this coin, there is silver in the bust: resilience. Resilience to environment and people. Resilience to highs and lows. However, with this armor of resilience comes the inability to trust others or to allow love in. If trust and love aren't coming in, then they certainly aren't going out either.

The second heaviest weight a person can shoulder is this damn suit of resiliency that keeps good, healing, and self-love energy from getting in! Normal wasn't a word I used or considered to be within my vocabulary back then, mainly because I didn't have a clear definition of what "normal" was. Normal to who? Normal to me didn't contain any good, only more numbness. I felt mentally old and weathered, with forecasts of bleakness and disappointment to come.

Back on the home front, my relationship with Jeanne had become cold and distant, as had every relationship in my life. If you served me no purpose, then we were no more than a current convenience to each other, and Jeanne accepted this. We had a large enough house that worked for us. She could no more see the rest of our life as a couple than I could, so it was an amicable deal for both of us. Besides, I couldn't tolerate another Bob Marley tune, stoned or not, and that was certainly Jeanne's "one love" thing. Now I just chuckle at the memory.

That September, I abandoned the entire apple-picking season for mere lack of desire. After 12 weeks in a canvas Woodsman tent, comfortable or not, I wanted walls, my dogs, and autumn scents. I had already maxed out my earnings for EI stamps, so another month of grunt work would only leave me with a cider hangover and maybe $300 tops, so screw that idea. I would have the house and property to myself and hopefully the dogs – Bonnie and Clyde – for a month of nothing. I would visit the post office every few days and hike the bush out back or at the nearby spring.

One morning, while en route to wherever for whatever reason, who should cross my path but David. David always had this innate ability to enter a situation or scenario and 'adapt' immediately. He called it "machismo," and I called it ego.

As was customary after a length of time without breaking bread amongst friends, David insisted we feast and party, which were two words I was in complete agreement with. Having traded the Volkswagen Hippy Van for a 2-door Renault 5-speed, David jumped in the driver's seat, reached over and opened my door with his foot, then cranked Bob Marley. FUCK!!! I just can't get away from kumbaya and patchouli!!

Within maybe 15 minutes of navigating the crossroads, we entered the "Lac a la Tortue" neighborhood, which was a sheltered small lake moments from the main country road and minutes from the east end of the village of Grand Mere. I had meandered back here a few times with my truck, mostly lost in the road work, so I knew little of the area or development. In fact, I recall only one area with development around the entire lake, and not just because there was only one road.

David turned left onto what wasn't really a road and wasn't really a driveway either, and then maneuvered our way through the potholes to the end of the cul-de-sac and parked the car beside an unfinished wooden structure with several levels and numerous rooflines. As the surrounding property was quite wet, with little footpaths meandering in different directions away from the house, the entire dwelling was lifted by a four-foot cinder block foundation.

David insisted that I wait in the car until he requested entrance to the house from the inhabitants, Bo and Laurie. He wasn't even up the steps to the door when a slender blonde wearing a black miniskirt swung open the door and proceeded to embrace David. From where I was sitting, this blonde was older by a number of years but still pretty hot, all things considered. She quickly glanced over to see me waiting, then waved me in without hesitation. I wasn't quite sure why David was playing this gangster-type role when Laurie instantly embraced me with such a warm, full-body hug, like she had known me my entire life.

After a moment of warming up to each other by sharing a little background info, Laurie sat us down at a very large, handcrafted hardwood dining table and served us a cocktail of choice. Looking around the interior of this eclectic home, it was evident that it was not only built in stages but also by different tradesmen. In the center of the back dining room wall was a superb, vintage cookstove with polished chrome rails and fixtures, as well as white enameled casings. This was truly the feature of the entire first floor, bringing with it a fire-based warmth that only a stove of this nature could provide. Off to the back right, a 'wonky' staircase rose up one floor to a bedroom landing, then continued up again to the bathroom landing.

Laurie was born and raised in rural Quebec, had two daughters, and one grandson nicknamed Punky. Some years ago, Laurie's first husband, Gil, had passed away from an illness I didn't understand much about. The house was started by Laurie and her late husband, which would explain why construction looked inconsistent. Laurie went on to describe the simple life they created back then, almost off-the-grid, healthy living. After Gil passed, Laurie needed a source of income, as she could no longer be a homemaker and pay the mortgage and such. I began to understand why David acted suspiciously when we pulled up the drive. The entire street/ driveway was one property with six houses adequately spaced on each side, and the property owner was the local motorcycle club, the name and chapter of which I will omit from the story. As I had numerous dealings with clubbers in the past, some good and some not-so-much, I wasn't fazed by who owned what.

The clubhouse wasn't any further than 10 minutes away, and with all clubhouses of this nature, there was a bar within, though not legally, and a compound for the club's bikes. Laurie was hired by the club to tend bar as well as arrange the "entertainment" when neighboring members were in town, and this ensured that all of her living expenses were covered. However, this wasn't where the majority of the cash came from, as there was another aspect of this street she lived on that brought in a substantial source of income.

Each dwelling on the street housed a particular person for a particular reason. The farther down the street you lived, the more important you were. At the entrance was the current "Sergeant at Arms," and across from him were the "Soldiers," positioned here for security. Laurie's house was the "Stash House," across from her was the President, and next to him was the Vice President. There was one other house whose occupant had nothing to do with motorcycles but everything to do with pharmaceuticals. The club had a local dentist on their payroll, and his function was to provide Novocain through his dental practice. The Novocain would then be used to "cut" pure cocaine into a more diluted product – in other words, it was "stepped on."

I will admit that this was a brilliant business move on the club's part; first, they found a dentist who liked to indulge, then set him up with an endless supply on the house. The dentist became addicted to the point that he couldn't imagine quitting, and both parties won. In this neighborhood, everyone had a purpose and a reason for being there.

As for Bo, Laurie's current husband, Laurie had met him at a club function a couple of years back while he was up visiting Quebec from Massachusetts. The two of them hit it off relatively quickly. Laurie urged the club to accept Bo as a new "Striker," or initiate to the club, and Bo simply didn't leave Canada. What I couldn't wrap my head around was why an American, non-French-speaking, lone biker would visit a rural community in Quebec with no intention of leaving. My gut said that Bo was a fugitive from the law because there is no way any enforcement bureau would anticipate a move like this. Besides, it's exactly what I did.

Laurie was just serving up our third beverage when a giant of a man walked in the door. Either the doorway was too low, or this behemoth was that tall as he ducked when crossing the doorway. Dirty blonde hair covered by a leather "Southern Rebel" hat tilted slightly to the right, leathers that looked like they had seen their share of road rash, tattered jeans, and scuffed black engineer boots adorned this stereotypical badass biker. Laurie rose to her feet to welcome Bo home with a kiss and embrace, then turned to introduce me. Extending a hand the size of a catcher's mitt, Bo engulfed my hand with a rigorous handshake and welcomed me to his home.

The more we talked, drank, and smoked, the more Bo, Laurie, and I began to gel. Maybe it was because I was English, like Bo, in a place where we were literally alone, or maybe there was some sincerity involved. David and I spent the rest of the afternoon and evening with the couple, and I would return the next day to help Bo with some work around the house. I could sense that David had become uncomfortable the night before as Bo and Laurie were more interested in me than in him, which is why I presume he didn't accompany me back the following day.

Over the following weeks and months, I would spend more time with Bo and Laurie than I did with Jeanne or David. David had dropped out of the picture once again, and Jeanne had found a new love, which made me very pleased. I knew him from our planting contracts and found him to be very amicable, which was perfect for Jeanne, plus he loved Bob Marley! I now had reason to believe that we could share the house while having separate lives. Jeanne's family, however, wasn't of the same belief as they were very firm on their Catholic convictions. Jeanne didn't pay them any heed as she was more Rasta than any organized religion.

For the fall and winter months, I had secured employment at a local dairy farm, milking cattle twice a day – 6 a.m. for a couple of hours, then back at 5 p.m. It took a bit for me to get the whole squeeze-and-squirt rhythm down, but when I did, I had become quite proficient. This provided me with a little extra coin in my jeans, fantastically fresh cream and milk as I pleased, and an avenue to keep me busy. Being a part of the birthing process was a miracle I thoroughly enjoyed, but being 'buffaloed' into the stall wall by an uncooperative cow or smoked in the side of the head by a tail laden with solid cow nuggets wasn't; it was like getting a glass marble shot at the side of your face! I swear I could sense the cow laugh when she did it.

Although Laurie was in charge of cutting and bagging the cocaine rocks the club brought in, Bo and I refrained from indulging, at least in the beginning. Bo simply didn't enjoy it, and I was happy with my weed and hashish, which I had an endless supply of. Bo told me he did coke back in Massachusetts but stopped because he became too violent. I think this had something to do with why he left the state and fled the country. I couldn't imagine nor wanted to imagine this man violently strung out, as he was intimidating enough when he was straight.

As our friendship grew stronger, Bo felt comfortable sharing another side of him, a very paranoid side – weapons. In every room of the house, the garage, the attic, the crawl space, and several stashes in the surrounding woods, Bo had some caliber of gun. From lever action to shotgun (mostly sawed-off stock and barrel), .22 caliber, and every rifle gauge you could think of. He even had several hand grenades strategically placed leading up to the house. The one that really caught me off guard was the .22 caliber, double-shot Derringer stuffed in a hanging ivy plant in the bathroom above the tub. I felt 'privileged' that he had this kind of trust in me while being absolutely terrified at the same time. It wasn't long before I understood why he had the property set up as a fortress.

It was an early spring morning, and I had slept over the night before, occupying the couch, as we three had consumed far more than would allow any normal human being to function, more or less stand up.

A thundering "BOOM" followed by the shrill of a resounding alarm came from outside the house. Bo and Laurie came racing down from their bedroom, picked me up from the floor as it so startled me from my sleep, and we cautiously exited the house by a hidden trap door behind the couch. Across the street, the club president stood ranting and waving his fists, cursing in terms I didn't quite understand but am sure meant "motherfuckers" in guttural French. Within moments, every clubber on the street was there rallying for retaliation. Girlfriends, children, strikers, everyone, including me, were scurried into whatever vehicles were available, and we all took refuge at the clubhouse in town. Even the self-loathing numbness and disassociation I had developed towards every moment of my pitiful existence could not have prepared me for this!

The clubhouse was more of a compound than a gathering place. Twelve-foot-high cinder block walls with a massive electric reinforced gate enclosed the back-alley entrance of the facility, while the front of the compound appeared as a rocker bar with the club shingle above the front door. I wasn't given a choice to be there or not, for the club regarded me as an extended member of the family due not only to my association with Laurie and Bo but also to what I knew and was privy to by the club. Laurie and I would spend the next 48 hours inside the barricade before being allowed to leave. I never slept a wink for at least the first 36 of them, as cocaine flooded my system in an attempt to keep me aware and alive.

Within the week, the club had discovered who had committed the offense. A neighboring chapter of the club in Trois Rivieres was having repercussions over territory with a much larger club, and I do mean massively larger, with roots in Montreal. One of the opposing club's strikers had thrown an explosive, presumed to be dynamite, through the president's front window as a warning to back off or succumb to an all-out gang war. Way more than I wanted or needed to know.

Late April had rolled around, and I was now preparing for the spring plant to commence mid-May around Lac Saint Jean. I was spending less time with Laurie and Bo, as spring chores at the farm were amping up for the season. I would visit when I could and even lied a bit to them, just to let them believe I was neither afraid nor abandoning them, though clearly, I wanted out, opposed to spending my farm earnings on coke.

One mid week day, I proposed to Jeanne that we have a "pre-plant" gathering in our backyard just before the tree line. I had gathered a sufficient amount of barn boards and other flammables from the spring cleanup at the farm that was sure to burn for at least 15 hours plus. Jeanne went about contacting our planting gang of friends, and I headed straight to Bo and Laurie's place. A gathering of this magnitude required some 'party favors,' and who better to supply them than the club?

I wasted no time dilly-dallying with Laurie, as Bo was on an 'errand' for the club, and I had no desire to be there alone with Laurie should he arrive unexpectedly. Not that anything was going on between us, but Bo had become over-the-top paranoid since the explosion. In Bo's world of thinking, the bomb was meant for him, and the US government was on his trail – not a head game I wanted to be involved in. Laurie mentioned that she had just received a fresh block of coke that needed to be cut and that I was welcome to take a few grams on the house, as long as I promised to invite her to my shindig. This was a no-brainer – two sachets in hand, the invitation off the end of my tongue, and tally-ho, I was away.

I started assembling the bonfire around 4 p.m., giving me ample time before sunset to create a masterpiece burn. My neighbor, a friendly yet quiet gentleman, was a member of the Quebec Provincial Police, so I already had everything required to host such an event. Water hoses, extinguishers, shovels, pickaxes, saws, and auxiliary lighting were all strategically stationed around the house, yard, and burn pit. Houses out here were 100 feet or more apart, and the crew coming over weren't party animals by any stretch of the imagination. These friends were more folk artists, musicians, and French hippy types, most of whom I expected to be gone or sleeping beside the fire before midnight. By 6 p.m., everything was set and ready to ignite. I slipped inside for a bite to eat and a cold beverage, then proceeded out back and torched the heart of the pile around 7 p.m.

Watching and admiring the breath of the flames slowly climbing and engulfing the tinders beneath was as magical as any rainbow you've ever seen. The fuel varied in species, age, processed or not, stained or painted, and density. Treated fuel gasped iridescent flames of orange, blue, and green, while dried barn boards roared orangey-red. Truly magnificent, if you're into that kind of thing.

Folks arrived every 15 minutes or so, and Jeanne and I gratefully welcomed them to our home base. The house had a cellar with an outdoor entrance, so I would pop downstairs for a puff of hash and a sniff or two, then rejoin the festivities. This went on until around 9 p.m. or so, at which point, higher than a zeppelin, I decided to wash away the dirt and grime from the day, change my outfit, and get prepared for the endless night. There was no shower in this old railway home of ours, just a claw-footed tub that came up to my neck. Neither Laurie nor Bo had shown up yet, so why not, I thought. Clothes in a pile on the floor, butt-naked into the steaming tub I went.

I had no sooner taken a dunk beneath the surface of the water to erase the smudge from my face when I heard a familiar raspy female voice beside the top lip of the tub whisper, "Kevin, I can see your naked body, and I like what I see."

Like awakening from a nightmare, both hands gripped the side walls of the tub, and I jerked myself up so my torso was above the surface of the water while my hands quickly moved to cup my groin.

"What are you so embarrassed about, Kevin?" Laurie growled in a sultry yet horrifying voice.

"I told you I would accept your invitation, and here I am. Are you not happy to see me, Kevin? I bought this new skirt and blouse just for you to see."

If ever I wanted to swirl down the drain of a tub and disappear, now was the time. Skirt? More like glorified panties with laced frill. Blouse? How about a camisole woven from black dental floss fitted loose enough to allow her pert nipples to suggest another desire of hers?

"I am so screwed" was all I could hear juggling around my brain because, stoned or not, now I had an erection, so there was no way I was getting out of the bubble-topped water. Flashes of Nancy and

Joe flooded my veins and into every cell of my body, but with the difference that I had not even conceived of any sexual fantasy with Laurie.

In a raspy low-pitched voice that only a seasoned French mistress could pull off, Laurie exclaimed, "Wayon, Kevin, levre toi et montrez-moi ton pisette" …. I'm positive this needs no explanation.

"Laurrie!! Laurrie!! Where are you?" a voice bellowed from outside. "Laurrie?"

"Tabernacle!! C'est Bo!! Cache toi, Kevin…," Laurie muttered softly.

Hide? Where the fuck was I to hide? This tiny bathroom had room for one person as it was, and Laurie was enough to block even the desire for escape. I rose to my feet, bubbles sliding from my naked body towards my knees, revealing everything, including my erection. Standing in the tub, all of me exposed from the knees up, the skin on my face tingling like burning flesh from fear mixed with embarrassment, I raised my right leg to step onto the floor, and there he was, occupying the entire bathroom doorway.

Decked out from head to toe in full leather garb, a scowl on his face like Al Pacino in "Scarface" when he finds his best friend with his sister right before he blows his guts out, Bo latched onto Laurie's arm with his baseball mitt-sized hand and threw her from the bathroom onto the kitchen floor like a crumpled piece of paper.

"Get your ass in the truck, NOW!!"

Turning to see me piss myself all over the floor for an accounting I had no part in creating, Bo stepped aside from the doorway and allowed me to pass without a word spoken. Body shocked into fight, flight, or freeze mode, cortisol running rampant through every cell, I stiffly walked through the kitchen, but instead of turning right towards my bedroom, I bolted like a gun-shocked rabbit through the screen door, leaping in one bound from the porch onto the driveway and ran like I'd never run before – soaking wet and naked.

I fled for my life to the end of the road, around the corner, and just kept running. No shoes, and not a stitch of clothing, I stumbled through the back ravine, falling face first into the icy creek bed. Overdosing on adrenaline, I scurried up the creek embankment and cached behind the boughs of a juvenile cedar tree.

Hyperventilating was slowly replaced with just sheer panic and vomit. Alone in the darkness, body covered in mud and cedar bracks, I knew I had to go back to the house lest I freeze to death in the brush. Calming myself down as best I could, I stumbled my way through the darkness, eventually finding the path that I had created from walking Bonnie and Clyde. The soles of my feet shredded, shins and thighs scraped from the brambles lining the ravine, I came to see a glimmer of light down the trail. The closer I came to the threshold of our yard, the slower I stepped through the darkness. The fire before me blazed a torrent flame at least 8 feet high or greater.

Standing just beyond view of our guests, I mustered the courage to advance forward. As if in a march, eyes straight ahead, arms down to the sides, I progressed straight through the crowd, past the bonfire, up the front step, and into the house. Not a peep was mentioned as I broke through the cluster of guests, though every eye was on my back and naked ass. No one followed me into the house, and no one made a move to help me. I locked myself in my room and cowered in the corner, lights out, well into daylight the following morning.

Maybe it was noon when I opened the door, maybe it was late afternoon, it didn't matter. Not a soul was present inside or out. The scatterings of empties, ashes, blankets, and dinnerware were all collected and removed out of sight. Even my mind was 'clean' of any and all thoughts, numb to the environment I found myself in. Still nakedly raw and battered from the night before, I poured another hot, sudsy bath and escaped behind the bathroom door. I remained in that room for the remainder of the day and night, leaving everything of the night before in the mud and tears, blood and puke smattered upon the floor, vanity, toilet, and lower walls. The only important question now occupying my thoughts was, "What clothes shall I wear to my own murder?"

There was nowhere I could run or hide, no place I could take refuge from what was inevitable – a confrontation with Bo. If I was going to be beaten to death, shot, or simply left for dead somewhere in rural Quebec, this I chose to accept from the front and not some kind of attack without control. I kissed Bonnie and Clyde repeatedly about the head, prayed I would see them again, then mounted into my old Chevy pickup and headed south towards Lac à la Tortue and Bo.

Not halfway there, along a single-lane back road literally in the middle of nowhere, a familiar vehicle heading towards me slowed to a halt and stopped slanted across the gravel, maybe 50 feet away. The vehicle was Laurie's, though there was no Laurie as a passenger or driver. The driver's door flung open, and the compression of the shocks on one side of the car from the body weight of the driver released as the 6'6" behemoth stepped up, out, and away from the vehicle. It was Bo, and to my surprise, he carried no weapon or firearm … not that he needed one.

Not only was my heart in my throat, but so was a mouth full of bile that I couldn't bear to swallow, nor wanted to appear weak by spewing all over my boots or his. Too late—out it came as I crumpled over to one knee upon the gravel road, one hand hitting the ground, keeping me from falling face-first into my own puke. Bo drew closer, reached down to grab me by the scruff of the neck, and lifted me to my feet with one pull.

"Well, that was quite the fucking surprise. My wife gawking over your scrawny naked body in the bathroom. That fucking bitch!"

Standing speechless, praying silently that whatever he had planned would be quick and done with, I awaited the undeserving punishment and torture.

"I'll bet you never saw that coming, did you? You shot off so quick I never had a chance to speak with you. Where the fuck did you go, Kev?" Bo questioned me, calm and collected.

Feeling like I had just been hit without actually being hit, all I could retort with was, "Uh?"

"You vanished so abruptly that after I made sure Laurie was secured in the truck, I couldn't find you anywhere. Your friends said you took off naked, hysterical, down the road. I wanted to apologize for Laurie's behavior and…"

I never heard a single word from that moment on. Bo, apologize to me? Was I delusional or still wasted from the night before? Nothing was registering other than the stench of vomit clogging my nostrils. It was like all the sound had been muted, and just the visual of Bo calmly talking to me with the odd chuckle interjected. And then it was over. Bo wrapped me in a bear hug, gave me a rigorous shaking, turned around, and left. The dust from the parting vehicle soon dissipated around the distant corner while I stood trembling in the center of the road. Tears instantly flooded my eyes, and again I dropped to the stony road, but this time to both knees.

Without even the slightest inkling of what had just transpired, I lifted myself up, turned, and while trembling like a leaf in the wind, crumpled into the driver's seat, started the truck, and went immediately home.

I released Bonnie and Clyde from their compound, stumbled my way up the front steps, through the door, and headed straight for my bedroom. I collapsed face-first onto the futon lying in the center of the floor and awoke the next midday, Bonnie and Clyde lying protectively along both sides.

That was the last time I ever saw Bo, and from the whispers I heard from the tiny community over the following days, Bo had beaten Laurie quite severely that night after leaving my house. The last whisper I heard was that Bo was never seen again, alive or dead, after the story scattered around Lac à la Tortue.

The next couple of weeks came and went extremely fast, probably because I kept very busy prepping for the plant. In hindsight, the 'busyness' was to keep my mind away from both chaos and fear while ensuring I was able to leave, or flee, at a moment's notice. The first plant run would be in "Blueberry Country," as it was nicknamed, or Lac Saint Jean, to be correct.

This area was well known for pine flats and a sandy substructure, a haven for explosive blueberry yields after a fire or clear-cut. Clearcutting pine, though deemed catastrophic to some (tree huggers, that is), was the closest method to natural fires for harvesting timber. The cones of the pine required extreme heat to open the bracts and allow the seeds to fall, while the flame cleared the underbrush, exposing the fertile ground to receive the seeds.

Blueberries were the natural symbiotic species to create new ground cover through rapid growth, while the pine seeds took root and started to grow. These blueberry-laden sand flats were so dense you could 'rake' the plants with your fingers, collecting marble-sized berries by the handful! And intensely blueberry-licious with flavor? Smucker's All-Natural Jam had nothing on these berries!

Our job was to ensure the best density of pine seedlings per acre, and of all ground types to conquer as a planter, these were the best sites. For Richard and me, we could knock out $300/day each before lunch, and honestly planted. The company knew exactly how to get the crews gangbuster ready for the season by throwing easy cash our way because immediately after these grounds, we would head to moss and bog-heavy grounds that could and would swallow you alive if you stepped off the rolled furrow. We're talking floating mats of moss prepped for planting by machines with pontoon tires 8 feet high by 4 feet wide. The attachment pulled behind would cut and flip the moss over much like a plow drawn behind a tractor, or in the case of rural Quebec, a draft horse. Richard and I did quite well on these sites, but we also knew that to make it pay and do so safely, we planted side by side as opposed to starting end for end, respectively. A planter need only step or stumble aside once to experientially know NEVER to allow it to happen again … ever.

The base camp was already established on a deactivated landing with only a few installations to be completed, like hot water showers, latrines, and secured waste storage. Our "go-to" handyman was an awesome fellow named Guy (pronounced Gee) I had met briefly over the winter months while visiting a friend of a friend's house just north of Grand-Mère, a sweet petite lady named Lucy. Lucy was the highest-demanded and highest-paid camp cook in the entire company. Lucy was 5' nothing and not a hair taller, and weighed maybe 90 lbs., most of which was her smile and charismatic charm. Lucy was an absolute doll, the type of lady you just wanted to hug and never let go.

As Richard, Jeanne, and I were among the first to arrive at base camp (this way we got the best tent locations for our personal sites), we all pitched in to help Guy finish off the necessary installations. While securing water lines for the showers, I heard a voice approaching from across the landing, a voice that sounded raspingly familiar. I paid no heed and returned to tightening the remaining hose fittings, then took a seat atop the toolbox.

Suddenly, I was poked in the ribs both sides from behind, which startled me off my perch and onto the dusty ground. I am very ticklish in the ribs, and whoever pranked me knew this.

"Alloh, Kevin!! Did you miss me? C'est fait longtemps depuis j'ai te vu."

Instantly my heart pulsated in my throat, almost gagging me to the ground—the voice belonged to Laurie.

I picked myself up from the dust and swatted away the debris from my jeans. How in the …? Why the …?

"Laurie, what on earth are you doing here? Did you know I would be with this camp and crew?"

Laurie went on to explain that Lucy and Guy were not only dear friends but also very, very valuable customers of hers. Laurie was also personal friends with the owner of the company and most of his crew bosses. These friends were longtime customers of the club's cocaine business, and as Laurie was their supplier, she knew where I would be all along. The question became, "Was she here for me personally, and if so, why?" The whole thing freaked me out, so I made the normal pleasantries with her, then went about my business.

This first contract was completed in under 10 days, so we were given a bonus just to keep us pumped about the next run. Laurie stayed with Lucy and Guy for three days, helping out with her exquisite cooking skills where she could, and stopping by my place at the dinner table now and again. She didn't push or force a conversation regarding the last time we saw each other, and I made no conscious effort to look for her when I got back to camp. The day she left for home, she had waited until breakfast was finished and we were loaded off to plant, which was typically around 4:30 a.m. She had left without notice or goodbye, but upon returning to my tent at the end of the day, I found a handwritten letter and a small sachet with 2-3 grams of coke in it.

It took the better part of an hour to open her hand-crafted envelope and read her words, as I had expected something that I didn't want in my life or awkward circumstances between us. On the contrary, Laurie apologized for her behavior and went on to explain the abuse she suffered at the hands of Bo and how she couldn't tell the club for obvious reasons and that she really did love him and so on. I understood everything she said, even in French. Battered and abused women, more often than not, do not speak up, do not fight back, do not leave, and under no circumstances tell someone else. This holds true to this day.

What Laurie did find in me from the day we all met was an ear that listened and heard, a heart that welcomed without judgment, and an embrace that always said, "I care about you." To this day, I still embrace people close to me with a welcoming bear hug that says, "I care." This has never changed in me. Laurie found in me what she couldn't find in Bo, and Bo knew it. She went on to explain that Bo held nothing against me for being me, as he found the same qualities in me as Laurie did, just attuned to him and his nature. This was why he never beat me or murdered me there in the middle of the dusty road. He did, however, beat Laurie within breaths of her life. She closed that segment of the letter with, "He'll never bother or beat me again." I chose to let that statement slide away like diarrhea.

Laurie asked, without expectation, if we could and would remain friends, and that when she came to supply the camp with 'essentials,' we could share a coffee or stroll and talk in the picturesque surroundings. This I was open to.

It was still early, so I went to see Lucy to let her know that when she speaks with Laurie next, that I agree to her terms of friendship. Lucy produced a smile that only she could, knowing exactly what I was referring to. I parted the tent and walked with a sense of peace back to my camp and went to bed.

CHAPTER 13

The Quebec planting season typically ran from early May until late August, which for most of us ensured we had the employment stamps to collect Employment Insurance throughout the winter months. This particular season seemed to fly by, most likely because I now had an endless supply of 'free' cocaine. Laurie would come to camp or the nearest village to the new camp, as we relocated every 3-4 weeks, and then spend 4-5 days visiting. Halfway through the season, 2/3 of the entire crew were partaking in Laurie's narcotics, myself included.

I presumed that I had the best arrangement of all as I never spent a dime for my share of Laurie's narcotics. In fact, I got to cut, measure, and bag the powder before anyone even had their first sniff. Even this process allowed me the 'pleasure' of getting high on Laurie's dime. I had become so blinded and naïve to what was really going on while this beautiful blonde coyote of a woman enjoyed every sniff and puff of watching me fall. By the end of the season, Laurie and I were joined at the hip. I was her errand boy, dealer, and runner, but not her bitch or boy-toy.

Laurie would run everything by me first—every deal or manipulation, even right down to the slinky clothes she would flash. Laurie always had cash, and lots of it. She treated me like gold, even flaunting me off to some incredibly gorgeous dancers from the club's strip joint. Laurie would never allow any touching on their part or mine, and I respected her enough that it was never part of my agenda anyway. I appeared to have it all: cash, an endless supply of narcotics, a beautiful woman to hang from my arm, freedom to come and go as I pleased, respect among the members of the club, and one more thing—a harrowing addiction to cocaine.

Every day I was high on something, not necessarily cocaine. Hashish, weed, mescaline, alcohol, and cocaine were always readily available for me and free. Heroin or needles always freaked me out though, so I abstained from them. Thinking, "Those people are junkies," was a means of justifying in my mind why I avoided them. Who was I kidding? I was a junkie. For the next two years, I lived under the 'umbrella of Laurie.' At some point, something had to give, or break, or collapse.

It was a dismal, dark, rainy April eve, and we had just returned from Laurie's shift at the strip club. Completely wired for sound, pupils dilated like blackened pennies, I stoked the wood stove for heat and dropped all my clothes on the floor. Standing butt naked, face to the heat and ass towards the kitchen, Laurie suggested I draw a bath and she would finish up the night's count with Chantal, one of the dancers spending the night. As if the world around me had become invisible, and I to it, I sauntered my naked ass up the stairs, hesitating at each stair tread to pose, flexing and stretching in front of the floor-to-ceiling mirror, then nonchalantly stepping over the tub wall and into the empty soaker tub. Not a drop of water pursed the faucet, not a bubble, not a drip, not anything at all but me lay sprawled on the floor of the tub. The world around me didn't exist—I was that high. No sounds other than the voice in my head and the heartbeat behind my eyes, nothing at all…

A spider plant dangled above me, encapsulated in a macrame web of wool that supported the pot. This plant was more than just another of Laurie's indoor garden friends, for it held a dark secret. Strands of 'spiderettes' floated in mid-jump, held suspended by a mere thin translucent green thread. It was an ecosystem alone to itself while hiding the most dangerous of threats laying just below the rim of the pot. I lifted myself to stand and reach overhead, fingertips barely able to collect the secret. Sensing a successful capture, I closed my hand around the tiny object, hiding it from sight, and returned to lounge along the tub floor.

Calling out to Laurie and receiving no reply, I presumed that she and Chantal had retired for the evening. Looking to the miniature window clock, I realized it was close to 3 a.m. and that I had lost all perception of time. Wrapping myself in a towel, though not even wet, I descended the stairs down to the kitchen, pulled on my pants—only my pants—and sat alone at the giant dining table. Raising my hand above the tabletop, I released my clench and allowed the object to drop to the table. With a small and silent 'thud,' the double-shot Derringer pistol now lay before me.

Polished chrome, over-and-under barrels with an ivory Scrimshaw handle, weighing just over a pound if that, I dazed and admired this fine piece of pistol art, though it taunted me, calling me to caress it, grip it, aim, and squeeze the trigger…

Snapping out of this almost erotic dance-like trance with the pistol, I backed away from the bench seat and moved around to the back of the wood stove and removed a small river rock placed loosely in the hearth. I retrieved a sandwich bag full of snow-white crystalline cocaine, freshly ground from the night before, and sat back down at the table.

"Maybe if I have more coke…" I thought to myself, "…it will straighten me up."

Picking a teaspoon from the coffee server plate mid-table, I sprinkled a heaping load in front of me. The hardwood tabletop boards were lacquered with heavy plastic, making it easy to chop, spread, re-chop, and create perfectly formed 'snowbank' lines. Taking a crumpled hundred-dollar bill from my jeans and rolling it into a tube, I immediately loaded my right nostril with the first track and laid the bill aside.

"That should do it," the little voice declared.

Now starting to sweat, hands trembling, leg shaking, and heel tapping the floorboard, "Twist a spliff, Kevy, that'll do it," whispered again the now 'floating outside voice.' "A little spliff won't do much; go ahead, Kevin, just one more little hit."

Reaching for the pack of "Export Rolling Papers" resting next to the ashtray, then stripping away the paper from a cigarette, I sprinkled a small pinch across the centerline of a rolling paper. Once again taking my Desjardins Bank card to cut out a sizable track of coke, close to a quarter gram worth, I delicately placed the coke atop the tobacco, then twisted up the spliff.

Sparking the smaller twisted end of the spliff and allowing the first bit of paper to burn off and the tobacco to ignite, then waiting for the color of smoke to turn from greyish-white to a brilliant bluish-white, I pursed my lips around the blunt and inhaled through my mouth as deeply as I could until my head felt 'full.' Holding it in, then one last quick suck of air, hold and release. Dead silence, no voice, just heart thumps—very rapid heart thumps.

My brain felt larger than the cavity in my skull.

"Thump, thump, thump," my heart beating against the inside of my skull.

Standing and staggering back from the table, vision completely fuzzy and blurred, arms and hands raised in front, feeling around for objects as though blinded, vertigo… nausea… darkness… falling… silence… floating…

I recall looking down from just below the ceiling to see my motionless body crumpled and flushed in color, sprawled out on the couch and floor below. There was no sound, no movement, no breath or rising chest, and no animation anywhere—just dead silence and frozen time.

And then I heard the words, "Be heard, release your secret, go home and be seen."

A shock-like wave ran through me like a tsunami, and my upper body forcefully jerked up and into consciousness, into animation, into life, and with me in it. I was instantaneously transferred from the ceiling back into my chemical-laddened body.

Hyperventilating and trembling uncontrollably, my entire being started to wail with grief. Frantically and haphazardly knocking about the dining room, my trauma-stricken body raced to open the front door. Fumbling to release the deadbolt, I flung the door open, bare-footed, tripping over the door sill and crashing my way down the steps, face-first into the muddy puddle below. The rain had never felt so cold, and I had never felt so dead but alive at the same time.

I knew what the whispered words were referring to, though didn't know where they came from. The terrible burden I had been crucified with since Philip's death had to be released, and it had to be done now.

The wailing tears of guilt and shame transformed into mourning tears of childhood fear and remorse. I had suffered this cross of martyrdom for close to 14 years, keeping silent and barely seen like good children do. There was nothing left of me that resembled life, health, love, or spirit. Nothing further could be taken away as I had already been stripped and violated of everything that makes a person human, and furthermore, loved. I had nothing to lose. I could no longer uphold the vow to be silent.

Ignorant of the time, though not really caring, I carried my spiritless frame back into the house, picked up the receiver of the phone, and began to dial. On the third ring, a familiar yet unwelcoming voice answered the phone.

"Hello? Who is this? Do you know what time it is?"

"It's me, dad, I'm coming home."

I don't recall much of the remainder of that day after my crash from the overdose. The vague yet daunting glimpse of floating above my corpse was enough to break an invisible iron shackle that enslaved my ability to be an 11-year-old traumatized boy who believed he had killed his younger brother on Good Friday.

I spoke little of the trauma from the night before with Laurie, but just enough for her to accept the need for me to go home to my family the following day. She never questioned why, but somehow I think she inherently knew why. Laurie made all of my travel arrangements, a combination of Greyhound Bus and Go Train, the journey to start the following morning. The next morning, Laurie drove me to the Metro Station in Montreal, and I boarded the bus with empty hands and my heart on my sleeve.

The ten-hour trip felt no longer than half of that, and at no point was I anxious or overwhelmed; at least not until I exited the coach to see my father standing before me in the crowd, scowled look on his face and hands clenched in his jacket pockets. Without a word mutually spoken, we crossed the parking lot, jumped in the car, and headed for the highway.

The confession I had quietly rehearsed in my head during the journey home was nowhere to be found, not so much as a syllable. Without further hesitation, I blurted it out, the poison I had carried since that tragic day years ago.

"Philip didn't fall on the tracks, dad. I was so scared that when I turned to run, I ran right over him, trampling him to the tracks and leaving him to die before I jumped. I murdered Philip, dad…"

And then the 11-year-old tears began to flow, followed by all of the years of horror from my teenage and young adult traumatized life.

No sooner said and done, my father swerved suddenly through the traffic, coming to a full stop on the curb of the highway. Turning to clasp my face in his hands, tears now streaming from his eyes, he declared:

"You were only 11 years old, son. You could not have known or done any better. You did not kill Philip, son. I am so grateful that I didn't lose you too, Kevin!"

We sat alone together, holding each other without any hindrance, parked along the side of the highway until the sobbing ended and we had no tears left to share. It was almost dinner by the time we arrived home from what should have taken less than half an hour.

Reliving this moment in my life and sharing it with you now still brings tears to my eyes, though not tears of sorrow, but tears of relief. This burden I carried for all those years could have been avoided if it wasn't for the instilled fear I had been unwillingly ingrained with since early childhood, the vow to "Be seen and not heard, don't speak unless spoken to," "Big boys don't cry." These were family vows I was ingrained to commit to for me to "be a good boy."

When we arrived home, my mother was waiting for us in the front living room. I'm unsure what she had expected to happen, but I am sure it wasn't my truth. The three of us sat close together on the couch as my father explained what had transpired on the drive home. Once again, the tears and sobbing began to flow and continued to flow well into the evening as we openly talked and listened to each other for the very first time since the accident. That evening was the most restful sleep I had experienced in over a decade.

The next morning after breakfast, dad and I went outside to talk and smoke—he his cigar and I a cigarette—when he calmly informed me that he knew all along exactly what happened up on the trestle that day. As it was, after I gave my accounting of the accident, I was released and taken from the courtroom. The person next to take the stand was the train conductor, and he had given an exact occurrence of the events atop the train trestle that Good Friday, 1975. My father knew the entire time, for the past 14 years, that my reckoning was a lie, a fabrication, and yet he said nothing. Again, he reiterated that at the tender age of 11, my little boy mind couldn't have been expected to know anything more than fight, flight, or freeze, fight being an obvious unviable option. So given only flight or freeze, flight it was. He never questioned why I didn't tell the truth, though I offered my reasoning anyway. I told him that I didn't want to get into trouble, to be a "bad boy," that keeping my silence was what I was supposed to do. I just didn't want him to love me any less. By following the path created because of my silence, trauma after trauma would and did ensue. In the end, the silence had to be voiced.

After several days with my family, I returned to rural Quebec and Laurie, except this time without the indulgence of drugs. During those days in Ontario, we had discussed my future, and further education was again on the table. As I thoroughly enjoyed the outdoors and even the arduous lifestyle of a tree planter, attending a local college to study Forestry was very enticing to me, so I contacted Sir Sanford Fleming College of Natural Resources in Lindsay, Ontario, and requested an application be mailed. As the deadline for submissions for the upcoming Common Semester in September had passed, the counselor I spoke with expedited the application to me after hearing my story. She asked me to include a letter to the Dean outlining why I wanted to return to school and that I be accepted as an Adult Student. At the beginning of each school year, the college granted a handful of acceptances to adult students based on their desire, means, and necessity. Within a week, the application arrived, and within the same week, I had couriered the completed requirements to the Admissions Office. Now all I had to do was wait.

CHAPTER 14

With the Spring plant arriving in just a few short weeks, I put my "Boy Scout" hat on and began preparations. After 5 years of planting in every kind of weather and in some of the most daunting environments, I had put together a living quarter that provided as much comfort as could be expected outside of living in a cabin.

My 'home' was a heavy-gauge canvas Woods brand six-person tent with reinforced structural poles, guidelines, and pegs, and a custom-built (by me) front 'boot room' where I could shed my clothes and gear for the night in a dry, warm enclosure. No home was complete without a doormat, so I had a slip-proof rubber mat that I created from a salvaged piece of rubber from the farm.

The zipper of the front door I had replaced with a galvanized heavy zipper that always moved effortlessly and never rusted. There's nothing like trying to unzip a tent in the middle of the night to go to the bathroom and having to fumble with the zipper! A good rubdown with a beeswax candle when setting up camp ensured easy gliding when I needed it most.

Once inside, I had an elevated bed made up of a thick futon lying on a 3/8" sheet of plywood supported by milk crates. The crates were used as storage for the trip up, camp moves during the contract, and the final trip home. With feet to the door and head to the back wall, I had a small bedside table with my six-volt battery lantern, flashlight, and other small items on top. To the right of the table was my wardrobe. Using sturdy branches found while clearing my homestead, I would peel the bark to make sure there were no little critters hiding beneath, then lash them together to form a hanging rack. Having brought hangers from home, all of my clothes were off the tent floor where they remained dry and free of spiders. I also had a raised rack for my casual footwear; it only takes one incident of finding something undesirable sleeping in your shoes to take precautions so that it doesn't happen again.

As for heat during the cold Spring nights, an assortment of blankets combined with a kerosene heater was sufficient. If you've ever seen a tent go up in flames, especially the nylon-type dome tents, it's enough to put the fear of burning to death as the tent melts your face and body into the survival part of your brain. I make It a habit to burn only enough to warm the tent until going to sleep, or during rainy times to keep not only the tent warm but also to keep my clothes dry. A lot of humidity is created when living in a tent, as any experienced camper will admit.

Outside the tent, at least ten feet or so away, is my campfire. Having brought an iron grate from home, another salvaged item from the farm, it would rest on top of the river rocks I gathered nearby. Every camp always had a steady flowing water source on-site for obvious reasons, but also for forest fire protection measures. A short distance from the fire, I would create a clothesline between two mature trees, so as not to bend with applied weight, that I could hang out my blankets, towels, and clothes when needed.

All in all, I was living in comfort. This could be why many of the other planters came to my homestead because they knew it was a warm and inviting environment.

As our workday started with breakfast at 4 a.m., in the field by 6 a.m., then home by 4 p.m., we always had several hours to unwind and do as we pleased. For myself, I would retire for the night by 8 p.m., as I was always up by 3 a.m. and in the mess tent by 3:30 a.m. preparing my lunch. Richard held a similar morning routine, but he enjoyed staying up later and hanging out with some of his Quebecois friends.

Everyone in our crew, the six of us that planted as a team under one supervisor, Ghislaine, came to adopt a similar routine because they soon realized that Richard and I were the top-producing planters. We had become so proficient in our techniques that stashing wasn't necessary like it was in the early days. We still groomed the tangled mess of roots to accommodate the size and depth of the plantable hole, but that was it.

This season was special for me as I had my eye on a new prize— the acceptance into college and all of my own doing. I wanted no assistance from my family, nor did I want student loans; I wanted to prove to myself that I could do it under my own terms. For the first time, college felt so right, so perfect for me, and especially in the field of Environmental Sciences with a major in Forestry. In my heart and soul, I belonged to Nature and all of Her splendor. This is also why I have always, since childhood, felt a deep-rooted connection to Aboriginal Peoples. Inside, I felt that I was Native but born into a Caucasian family, thus having white skin. My mother used to kid with me that I was dropped off at the front door by a Native woman and left there to be raised. Today I know that there is a plot of land that I belong to, not that belongs to me.

The Spring contract flew by without a hitch, and we were taken back home for a week's break before heading north to the Abitibi area of Quebec. This meant sand flats for Pine, blueberries, muskeg for Spruce plugs, and massive moose. For Richard and I, it also meant big money. Our system of planting for these terrain types was perfected such that we rarely stood upright between trees as we maneuvered and moved that quickly. For this plant, however, I would not be stopping once I had achieved $150 of pay but pushing myself to double that and clear $300 for the day. And you know what? Between my desire and dream of returning to school and my successful planting method, most days achieved this and more. By the end of the plant, I had cleared $6000 in savings, which would be enough to cover tuition and books for the first year, along with enough for food and housing for the first 6 months. All I needed was to be accepted.

Laurrie came to visit during the final week and, of course, brought her rations of pharmaceuticals and narcotics. Laurrie also brought personal items for various staff, including the cooks, maintenance, crew bosses, several planters, and of course, myself. Toiletries and the like for most people, as well as myself, and I also had her bring rolling papers and a tin of Drum brand tobacco. While away in camp, Laurrie would also retrieve my mail from my post office box in Herouxville, where I lived.

On the day she arrived, everyone shared the usual pleasantries of camp life with her before she came to see me at the end of the comradery. With a smile that rivaled the starlit skies, she ran to embrace me and share her affections. Over the past few years, we really had come to love each other in a natural and enduring way regardless of the nastiness that brought us together.

"Kevin, regardes!!" she exclaimed while waving a vanilla-colored envelope in the air.

"C'est du l'école que tu as donné une application!"

My heart jumped right into my throat, and I buckled over at the waist with a nauseous feeling welling up inside. "This is it," I thought to myself, "What if I've been declined?" followed right after that. Rising up to take the envelope, then sitting down on a fireside stump, I reached into my pocket, took out my pocketknife, and sliced open the end of the envelope. Trembling fingers removed the folded response, then lifted it close enough to read aloud.

"Dear Mr. Hanna, It is with great pleasure that I inform you of your acceptance as an Adult Student into the September 1989 school year here at Sir Sanford Fleming College of Natural Resources, Lindsey Campus..."

I'm sure the shout-out that followed could be heard from miles away! Dropping instantly to my knees, tears of joy began to flow as I praised the heavens in gratitude. I didn't even bother to read the remainder of the letter because, in that moment, all that mattered was that I was accepted.

Laurrie approached me, tears also welling up, and raised me by the hand into her loving embrace.

"I am so proud of you, mon chou," she whispered in my ear.

Together we stood there in that loving embrace, parting slightly just enough to see the activated sparkle in each other's eyes, then back to hugging. That evening was now the second-best sleep I had experienced in the past decade plus.

The entire workday—from the morning routine, to planting, to the crew cab ride back to camp—passed in the blink of an eye. To my surprise and delight, Laurrie had shared my news with the entire kitchen staff, maintenance team, and crew bosses before I had returned to camp. Nothing out of the ordinary at first, but when I entered the mess tent after cleaning up, I was welcomed by the bellowing voices of the entire staff as they surprised me with "Félicitations, Kevin!"

Each and every person in the camp came to hug me, adorn me with kisses and well-wishes, then singing and dancing, and an entire celebration orchestrated just for me! I floated my way through the entire evening without so much as a sip or sniff or puff and reveled in the cleanest high a drug addict could imagine. I did not sleep a wink that night, my mind racing with dreams of personal fulfillment and the thought of moving home. It was like I had been reborn into a fresh and better life, and I was gratefully humbled for the transition and welcomed the transformation.

CHAPTER 15

Through sheer desire and inspiration, I was able to save enough funds to pay for my first year of college, as well as enough for food and lodging, based on shared accommodations with several other students, preferably adult students as well. Prior to the end of the contract, and on a daybreak into a local village, I had expedited the tuition bank draft via courier so as not to miss the deadline by assuming regular post would suffice. I hadn't, however, informed my parents. For this, I would wait until I had finished the season and was safely back at my home in Herouxville.

Upon completion of the contract, the company sponsored its annual celebration, which always lasted an entire weekend, all expenses paid. The last camp base was the venue, and no expense was spared in bringing up food beyond that of our regular work meals—steaks and roasts, legs of ham, a variety of freshly baked breads and cheeses by the wheel, and, of course, drink, and plenty of it! Beer and regular highballs if you chose, but also top-shelf liquors like Armagnac, Remy Martin, Ketel One Vodka, and Chivas Regal. Even the company owner, Guy, and his administrative staff would come for at least one night. If there is one thing Quebecois are exceptional at, it is celebrating! Two days of folk music, dance, food, drink, games, and all-around fun.

Then, just as quickly as the contract had started a few short months ago, everything had come to an end—camp packed, loaded, and hauled away—and we all went in our various directions home for another season.

Once at home, I didn't bother unloading the truck before I made my first call home, and not to my parents, but to my brother Stephen. Regardless of our relationship growing up, Stephen had been by my side on several occasions in my late teens and most recently a few years back when I had entered a severe depression after a cocaine bender that lasted several days. With just a phone call, he had dropped everything going on in his life and came to be with me. Deep inside, and without physical expression, I had always loved and admired my older brother because he was a different kind of role model for me, something I had never expressed openly to him.

When he picked up the receiver and spoke his usual greeting, I simply blurted out, "I've been accepted to college!" Confused, as I had not told anyone of my actions, he questioned me immediately about what, where, and most importantly, when. Then, without hesitation, he exclaimed, "Kevin, I'm proud of you. Give me a couple of days to arrange things, then I'll be right there to bring you home."

The mention of being proud of me meant more to me than anything that had ever transpired between the two of us. No one in my family had ever openly said this to me, especially my father, so it did carry a significant amount of value and weight. The open show of affection or adoration was definitely not an occurrence that happened in our household, not even between my parents—ever.

To do so would break one of the Cardinal Rules, the vows we all grew up with, most likely including my parents. Within the next 48 hours, Stephen arrived in Grand-Mère with an empty pickup truck and trailer set to help me create my new life. It was now time to phone home and share the news.

"Hello?" the soft voice of my mother answered.

"Mom, I'm moving to Lindsay. I've been accepted into the college there; Stephen is here with me now to bring me home."

What followed from my mother was a barrage of questions:

"What college?"

"What course?"

"When do you start?"

"Why didn't you tell us sooner?"

"Where will you live?" and so on. And then came my mother's tears of joy. Whether they were for having me closer to home, or for going back to school, or both, only she knew why, and it didn't matter to me why. The fact was that I was going back to Ontario, closer to my family, and starting down a new path in my life, one that I would blaze myself.

The conversation didn't last much longer than the time it took to answer her questions, mostly because my command of the English language had become quite lacking during the past five years, speaking only French, and Quebecois French at that.

That evening, Laurrie treated us to gourmet-quality crepes, topped with freshly shaved cured ham and Asiago cheese, garden-picked strawberries, freshly canned Maple Syrup, and homemade whipped cream. Amongst Laurrie's notable skillsets, traditional

French cooking was at the top, and both Stephen and I made sure that we had more than our fair share of these fabulous crepes that evening. After dinner, we sat and shared stories and embellishments until shortly after midnight before retiring to bed. Morning would come quickly, whether we, Laurrie and I, managed to sleep or not, and so it did.

For me, there's a big difference between saying "goodbye" and "see you later," or something to that effect. "Goodbye" is exactly that—finished, done, completed, not coming back. "See you later," or whatever version you use, is also exactly that—a commitment to see or visit or talk with another at a future point in time. Moving from Quebec to Lindsay, leaving everything and everyone behind in this move, was a "goodbye" to me, and I openly welcomed it. I would retain the good memories and good people I had met along that path, but I would cut the rest out, like trimming the fat from a cut of meat. What I didn't say to Laurrie during our last embrace, our last shared tears, was "see you soon." It was "goodbye" and everything that came with it, but this was not something Laurrie came to understand during the hours of conversation we shared the evening before. Maybe it was the incorrect use of words or phrases I used in my version of French during this conversation, I don't know. What I did know was that as Stephen and I drove off, my gut feeling was that this was not the last time I would see Laurrie.

Within several very short hours, we had arrived at Stephen's home in Napanee, Ontario. Here, I would store some of my belongings, such as my refurbished canoe and some handcrafted camping gear I had accumulated over the past 5 years. The fewer belongings I trailed along to my father's house or Lindsay, the better. Not that I had many personal belongings, as most of it was donated, given to friends, burned, or sold before leaving Quebec. The personal belongings I did intend to bring to college with me were things that held a very dear spot in my heart and soul, most of which I still have today, like a "Fire Stick" from a tribe in the deep Amazon Jungle that was given to me by David, and an "Alligator Trunk" from the early 1900s that I purchased at a secondhand store in Montreal. Priceless items to me, nonsense items to others.

Stephen and I stayed the night, then packed my necessities for Lindsay and headed out for Oshawa. My parents' house was a little over an hour away, which gave us some time to dream together about my future and the possibilities of where it may take me after graduation. My thoughts and dreams since early childhood all involved snowcapped mountains, wildlife large and small, vast tracts of unoccupied land, and Aboriginal Peoples, those that I felt connected to more than any other race or culture, including my own Caucasian Canadian British Loyalist heritage and the vows or beliefs it came with, especially the ones that crippled my view of the world around me and what I deserved to be, do, and have.

The closer we came to Oshawa, the tighter the knot in my stomach became, so much so that I asked to make a quick roadside stop along the highway. The TransCanada Highway has service stations conveniently located at designated locations, mostly for the big rigs that service the country, but for the common traveler as well. I had mentioned to Stephen the need to use the toilet for urinary reasons, although the reality was I needed to throw up, and quickly.

Flashes of past memories had been bombarding me for the past 20 miles or so, memories that I just couldn't shake. The underlying root message was the acceptance, or lack thereof, of my father. Even though we had our unveiling session of truth regarding Philip, there still lived and breathed the "good boy" requirements and vows that had been involuntarily ingrained in my "little boy" psyche when I was told several years past not to return home.

At the time when I moved away and was told "don't come back," my father had reached a pinnacle that most business-minded people could only fantasize about. Not only had my father become the sitting Lodge Master of the local Masons, but he had also achieved the corporate seat of Chief Executive Officer for Ackland Granger, Canada. This is the kind of power that comes with benefits like a flight on the Concord, round-trip first-class trips to five-star destinations with accompanying accommodations to places like Maui, and for the "wanna-be golfer," tickets to top-tier PGA tournaments in places like Greensboro, North Carolina. Truth be told, my father scared me—not for fear of physical abuse, but for never being good enough to meet his standards and approval.

Even before my life went into the shitter, I had never heard the words "I am proud of you, Kevin" part the lips of my father, regardless of what I had achieved. It was always my mother, bless her heart, who took the brunt of all my garbage but also gave what little she had to give to me along the way.

The definition of success that I had come to believe as gospel was entirely based on the level of achievements my father had created. This definition created numerous unconscious beliefs as well—success means no personal attention to family; to accumulate large sums of money involves leaving your family for extended periods of time, as well as missing milestone events, birthdays, and more. There are others that I'll leave for my next book, but the bottom line is that these were things I unconsciously hated, but consciously desired—the highest standard of success that my father lived. I hated what he did and who he had become, but I aspired to have what he had. It was a double-edged sword, one that cut me with both thrust and retrieve.

With gullet and gut cleansed, we parted the station for the final leg of the trip home. While approaching the driveway, Stephen laid on the horn, summoning my mother with open arms, welcoming her 'long-lost son' safely home. My father followed behind with a pleasant smile on his face and a welcome-home embrace. With all the welcoming short talk aside, we entered the house where the inundation of questions began. Stephen chuckled silently, embraced me like only a loving brother could, whispered again, "I'm proud of you, Kevin," walked out the front door, and drove off.

That evening was spent discussing the next two years of my life and the possibilities that followed upon graduation. I had made it quite clear that I neither needed nor wanted any financial support, though home-cooked meals once in a while would be greatly appreciated. I didn't want to have the feeling that I was indebted financially because I knew it would come with expectations of perfection on top of financial servitude. I chose to be my own self-made person, under my own conditions and efforts, something I would have thought my father could and would appreciate.

That Sunday morning, after church, we made our way to Lindsay, located my new accommodations for the next year, hugged closely, and parted ways.

To be continued...

SUMMARY

It's easy to place blame on others for our shortcomings and challenges in life, as it's part of our human nature and experience. However, there is a difference between blame and inherited qualities, characteristics, beliefs, and vows. Believing that the challenge or problem is someone else's fault communicates a wrongdoing of some nature, which, in most cases, could have been avoided. When a quality, characteristic, belief, or vow is inherited, it is not a personal and intentional act that is consciously imposed upon another. There is no vindictive or harmful intention behind the inherited subject, and more often than not, the inherited subject has been passed down from generation to generation without question.

To take this even further, we can break these subjects into physical and nonphysical. Physical is straightforward, as in the example of appearance. I look like my father, have the height of my father, and have physical health qualities like my father. My two siblings lean more toward my mother, with some qualities of my father. This is basic genetics and DNA.

The nonphysical takes into account that which is not completely visible to the naked eye, such as intelligence, humor, beliefs, and family vows. Of all nonphysical attributes that have a direct impact on the direction of a person's life, beliefs and family vows are at the top of the list. The difference between the two words, "belief" and "vow," may seem minimal, but in fact, this difference can lead a person to live a life filled with joy and abundance or a life doomed to setbacks and failures, traumas, pain, and suffering, and even to live an unfulfilled life in the shadows.

So, what is a belief? A belief is a firm thought or opinion that something is true and is usually based on revelation. An example is personal faith and religion. How many variations of religion are there? Which one is right? Beliefs can be obvious, or they can be hidden. Beliefs can also lead to habits. Look at smoking as a prime example. When I was a youngster, it was believed that smoking was cool and grown-up, that it helped concentration while relieving boredom at the same time. I know, it sounds ridiculous, doesn't it? Beliefs, for the most part, can be easily changed or replaced without much effort when the belief is scrutinized for what it is.

A vow, on the other hand, is a commitment or pledge to do something specific, to live a certain and specific way. It is a solemn promise or assertion by which a person is bound to an act, service, or condition. Vows can also be obvious and apparent, as in marriage vows, or hidden, as in a family vow passed down, which commits a person to be, do, have, or have not. Family vows, sometimes referred to as Tribal Vows, are implanted at the infancy stage by the caregivers and/or the environment to which they are exposed. These vows can lead to great heights, but they can also lead to shame, guilt, pain, and suffering.

Vows are affirmative, meaning that's just how it is without question. Of the numerous vows hidden within the human psyche, including mine, it is the family vow of "Be seen and not heard, don't speak unless spoken to" that directed my life experience in ways I would not have consciously chosen.

Have you ever wondered why you do the things you do? Have you ever ventured down the path of self-discovery or visited the "Self Help" section of your local bookstore? Chances are very high that if you are reading this book, the answer is yes.

"Think positive thoughts."

"Commit to daily affirmations."

"Create a vision board."

"Act as if."

"Be, do, have."

The list is endless. Sure, there is validity in these; however, if you have a Tribal Vow that is contrary to the above, the desired result will NEVER happen – period.

Affirmation – "I am so grateful that my bank account is overflowing with money."

Tribal Vow – "The love of money is the root of all evil."

Think about this for a moment. Where did this vow come from? Did you put it there, or was it 'given' to you? Money in and of itself is neutral and inanimate. Money has no feeling and is made of paper or metal. Money is a tool, nothing more and nothing less. If a person is already 'bad,' money will be used to bring out even more bad in the person. You can say aloud or write out your affirmation a bazillion times, but if you unknowingly believe that money equates to "sin" or "evil" or "bad" or any other negative impact or sacrifice, and you are a good person, you can have an income that far exceeds your needs and automatically create ways to get rid of it.

The self-help gurus often call these "False Beliefs," which obviously means they aren't based on fact. Another interesting thing about false beliefs is that the majority of times they are hidden in your psyche or Subconscious Mind. I have been a 'student of the game of life' for several decades now, and early on, when I kept hearing the term False Belief and that they aren't obvious and apparent, my question of "How do I know what they are if they are false and hidden?" kept coming back because none of the exercises worked for me. Tribal Vows will ALWAYS win over beliefs, be they apparent or hidden.

"You can have your own opinion, but you can't have your own facts."

Over the course of my life, religion as I was led to understand it didn't 'work' for me. My first conditioning experience with this was when Philip didn't rise from the dead after three days like Jesus did. Understand that I was going on twelve, and it was Good Friday when the accident occurred; that every Sunday, without question, we attended church. I couldn't not believe he wouldn't come back because I wasn't told the entire truth about life, death, and the afterlife. However, why would my parents even have the need to teach me these things at that age? So, come the third day when I awoke excited to see Philip back with us, only to find a home turned into a house, to find a happy family turned into five of six people living in sorrow and grief, my personal faith or belief cracked.

It wasn't until recently that I consciously chose to take a macroscopic look at life, then start looking for truths based on a microscopic approach.

These are my findings:

1.   Religion is the study of the Creator.

2.   Science is the study of creation.

3.   Metaphysics is the bridge that closes the gap between the two.

I am certainly not an atheist, as my personal relationship with my Creator is unwavering and undeniable. I am simply not bound to believe only in the words of the Bible. I will not declare myself as a religious person but most certainly as having three very distinct 'parts' to me.

1.   I have a body, which is not 'me.'

2.   I have a conscious entity that allows me free will, which I see as ego

3.   I also have the spark of life that is always with me regardless of what I do or say or think or feel, and that spark of life is inherent in every living being, great or small, on this planet; it's the spark that is the giver, provider, and sustainer of life itself. This is our direct connection to the Divine.

Nowhere in this statement above is there opinion. It is fact based on science, Molecular and Quantum Physics. It is no more deniable than the Law of Gravity.

Staying within the realm of Science and Quantum Physics, it is a fact that everything is energy, constantly moving into and out of form, never created and never destroyed, moving at different speeds or frequencies. We're born, we live, and then we die; pretty basic. If we go back a few thousand years and focus on Eastern beliefs, we are introduced to the energy centers found within the whole. Keeping this simple, as an individual, you are one 'big' energy source, and within that vibrating energy are seven smaller, yet infinitely powerful, governing energy centers called Chakras. I know, you may be thinking this is a little "woo-woo" or sacrilege against God or the like. I understand completely because I used to as well – it was "hippy stuff" to me. I am no longer of this belief (remember what beliefs are?).

These energy centers are developed as we progress from infancy to childhood, through youth, and so on. They are the Root Chakra, Sacral Chakra, Solar Plexus Chakra, Heart Chakra, Throat Chakra, Third Eye Chakra, and Crown Chakra. Their locations are, in ascending order, the base of your spine, groin, abdomen, chest, throat, between the eyes above your nose, and the top of your head. Their energetic colors, in ascending order, are red, fiery orange, yellow, green, sky blue, indigo blue, and purple/violet.

Through my own personal research combined with direct application of medically documented and accepted techniques, and then applied to my life experiences, this is what I have found to be true for me. Again, you are free to agree or disagree, though I advise that you do your own tests first.

For the purpose of this book and the understanding of the power of Family or Tribal Vows, we're going to focus only on the bottom five chakras: Root, Sacral, Solar Plexus, Heart Chakra, and Throat Chakra, as these are the first to develop.

So here you are, born fresh into a new world, a new life. Nothing is your own, not even your thoughts. You come with the fear of loud noises, and some say the fear of falling. You are completely dependent on your caregivers or parents for everything, primarily food and security. You come with nothing else; you have nothing else. Everything about you is immature and undeveloped. You are completely and entirely dependent upon others for everything.

As everything about you is undeveloped, including your ability to censor what goes into your energetic system, you absorb absolutely everything without prejudice – everything. You have no freedom of choice in the matter because, again, you are 100% dependent on your parents or caregivers. What they say, what they do, how they behave, what they believe to be Truth, everything is openly downloaded into your energetic system. There is no disqualifying these statements; these are facts. Think about it: at birth, we don't even come with the ability to control our own body "movements."

Now let's introduce the first energy center to develop, and this is the Root Chakra. This chakra is about safety, security, belonging, what is and isn't. It is rudimentary and your "early warning system." Its function is to keep you safe. When danger looms, this chakra sends signals throughout your entire body and nervous system. Cortisol is released in your brain, and you go into "Flight, Fight, or Freeze" mode. This chakra is the governing center of what you will be, do, have, and experience in life, without question.

Above this is your Sacral Chakra, and it is your creativity and nurturing center. It's the run and jump and "look at me" energy. It's about fun, magic, and dreams. At infancy, it is closed off and undeveloped.

Your Solar Plexus Chakra is about power and action. It's about movement, stepping up and out. Metaphorically, think "six-pack" abdominal muscles. Courage, strength, and forward motion.

The Heart Chakra is straightforward; it's about the ability to give and receive love. Some like to think of this chakra as red because red is globally accepted as the color of love. Have you ever seen a Valentine's that didn't involve red? Exactly. Green, however, is the color of life, and life is about giving and receiving love in a myriad of forms.

The last chakra we will introduce is the Throat Chakra. This is your power of speech, the power of creation through your spoken word. Your words are your thoughts, which are a form of energy as well as a form of prayer, that are sent out into the ethos around you.

The Root Chakra directly affects absolutely everything that does or does not happen in each of the chakras above it. It is the filter through which the higher chakras are 'fed.' The Third Eye and Sacral Chakras become more open and developed as we pass through life and through the development or awakening of what we really are.

In primal times, when we had the fear of being eaten or attacked by something big, ferocious, and nasty, little to no development of the Root Chakra occurred, and therefore, it was so for the other chakras above. Simply put, eat or be eaten.

Now jump ahead a few millennia, let's say to a time when the belief was that the world was flat. Again, not much development above the Root Chakra beyond those of higher means and education. To the commoners, they believed what they were told without question, including but not limited to religious beliefs.

Where I began to discover the root cause of my 'life challenges' was when I went back to the time of my great-great-grandfather and the British Loyalist background and history (late 1700s forward). It was not uncommon for parents to instruct their children to "Be seen and not heard," "Don't speak unless spoken to," "Money doesn't grow on trees," "It's rude to show affection in public," and so on. During my childhood, I heard all of these and more. The thing is, my parents didn't think these up on their own; they would have come from their parents and so on, back through the family line. It was the first, however, that was the most crippling. It sends a direct warning signal embedded in the Root Chakra that it is not OK to speak up. If we look at the Throat Chakra as the power of your spoken word, and any and all beliefs, behaviors, actions, and words are governed by your "early warning system," then we see that nothing will pass from your security center up through your creativity, action, and love centers to even remotely come close to being manifested.

Think of an hourglass and how it is 'pinched' in the middle. The size of the hole between the top and bottom of the glass determines the speed at which the sand passes, correct? Now think of your Root Chakra as that pinch in the hourglass, the bottom being your legs and feet and, above the pinch, your torso and head. Bear with me on this. Let's assume that energy passes up from the ground through your feet and legs, continuing through your waist into your abdomen, chest, and upward. If your waist is the pinch and it is closed or barely open, how much energy would pass through? Would it be fair to say that the larger the pinched opening, the greater the amount of energy that would pass through? Correct. The same holds true for your Root Chakra.

As we are developing infants, we are bombarded with information from all directions all the time. Again, we do not have the ability to censor what goes in because we haven't developed that higher faculty. Medicine and science state that we are pretty much 'programmed' within the first six years of childhood, meaning that our core beliefs are programmed for us. Within these years, we also begin to develop our ascending chakras, starting with the Sacral Chakra. Remember, this is the nurturing, creative, magic, pretending, run-and-jump chakra; the more open the Root Chakra is, the more energy and power the Sacral Chakra receives, correct? This same scenario continues straight up through to your Heart Chakra and Throat Chakra.

As simple and as innocent as these statements made by parents or caregivers to their children seem to be, they can and do have a direct impact on the direction of the child's life.

When I looked back over the veritable plethora of traumas, tragedies, and challenges in my life, the more evident the above began to shine through. I'm not placing blame on what was custom based on my generation and family background, I'm simply trying to shine a beacon on what may be the cause or hidden vow that stops you or someone you know dead in their tracks. Breaking a tribal vow would lead to danger or, worse, punishment from the tribe itself, and this could be seen as worse than the breach itself.

The biggest lie of my life could have been avoided, along with years of heartache and self-destruction, had I been able to speak up, speak the truth, but I couldn't physically do so based on this family vow of silence.

Nor could I speak up about the physical bullying in school since grade six, or the physical and sexual abuse as a teen. To lay in bed every night dreaming about killing myself until committing the offense. Or how about consuming copious amounts of drugs and alcohol in an attempt to numb the pain and silence the 'devil' inside; all could have been avoided.

Vows such as this can condemn a life to the inability to achieve things like higher education, or to go after the life partner that is really desired, or to ask for that well-deserved raise or promotion, or to write the book that could help thousands of others. It's no different than hobbling a horse so it can't run.

CLOSING

Uncovering these vows has been a blessing in many forms for me. Where once I believed myself to be a coward for all the things I could and couldn't do or say, I now see that I had more courage and strength than I could have ever imagined. To unknowingly pledge allegiance to such a formidable vow and then abide by it under horrific situations and circumstances took the heart of a warrior. Years of guilt and shame melted away, revealing a brilliance that had been there all along.

I'm not in a place to say that I've "arrived" or that my life is purely rainbows and butterflies (though I look for and discover such treasures daily), as I have ups and downs just like everyone else. What I am saying is that by releasing myself from this and numerous other vows and replacing them with vows I consciously choose to commit to, life has truly become a game of magic.

It is with my sincerest wish that through my trials, traumas, tribulations, and surrenders, you are able to find even the slightest shimmer of the brilliance that has always been with you.

I am only a whisper away....